FROM THE ORIGINAL FRENCH MANICURE TO GLOBAL BEAUTY BRAND

IT ALL STARTED WITH

PINK

To SCOTT MY FUTURE BANKER
HOPE YOU WILL ENJOY
READING MY BOOK

1/6/2020

FROM THE ORIGINAL FRENCH MANICURE TO GLOBAL BEAUTY BRAND

IT ALL STARTED WITH

PINK

JEFF PINK

For my family.
You mean everything to me.

And to Orly Pink for being the namesake and
partner in business and so much more.

CONTENTS

IT ALL STARTED WITH
PINK

1

I DON'T THINK THIS IS FOR ME

"I don't think this is for me. What do I know about women's hair care?" It's February 1975 and I'm sitting with my boss, Jack Sperling, owner of Jack Sperling Beauty Supply in Van Nuys, California. He's looking at me in that way he always has of looking at me—like he thinks I might be just the slightest bit crazy.

"Listen, Jack," I continue, before he has a chance to talk me out of quitting, "you're doing a wonderful job of teaching me everything about your business, but..." I shake my head.

I'm thirty-one years old and I'm still so far from where I thought I would be. Is this really what I'm going to do with my life? Sell hair care products? Counsel hairdressers and housewives on how to get the red out of their hair?

Jack pins me with his gaze. "You're wrong, Jeff," he says. "Work for me for ninety days, like we agreed. If you still don't think it's for you, I'll give you all your money back." His eyes twinkle. "I promise you, Jeff. You're going to love it."

Ninety days.

That was the agreement. I'm hesitant.

Jack is persistent. I give in.

I don't think I'm going to love it.

The first time I came to the United States, I landed in Livonia, Michigan. It was 1964 and I had just finished two-and-a-half years of mandatory service in the Israeli army. At twenty years old, I had my whole life ahead of me and intended to live it in America.

When I stepped off the plane and my feet touched the black tarmac, well, what can I say?

It was love at first sight.

America in the 1960s was everything I had imagined it would be and the exact opposite of Israel.

There was buoyancy to it, a lightness. Everything was clean and organized, and people were open to new ideas.

Compared to the ancient land of Israel, the United States was— and still is—a new country. I felt as if it hadn't yet had time to feel the burden of its own history.

To buy things in America in the 1960s was easy—from cars to kitchen appliances. People had money to spend and the economy was booming. I admired the little things in life here in the States: the way people spoke, the way I could keep my bicycle outside the house and it would still be there in the morning, the way people would wave me into traffic as though they were actually glad to let me go ahead of them!

In America, there was room to breathe—wide open spaces, flat plains, huge mountains and winding rivers that seemed to go on forever. Israel was a country no bigger than the state of New Jersey, and at that time much of the land was uninhabitable. It was a miracle in the desert, but its collective history had hardened its people in a way that seemed oppressive to me: wars to protect its borders; the remembrance of the Holocaust; people forced out of their birthplace for reasons beyond their control. This all added up to a country that felt stifled and sad to me.

I left Israel when I turned twenty and enrolled at Lawrence Institute of Technology (now known as Lawrence Technological University) in Southfield, Michigan, where I studied Industrial Management. I lived with my older brother David, who'd already made a life for himself and his family in Michigan. At that time, I didn't know exactly what I wanted to do, only that I wanted to do it in America.

But the American dream would have to wait. I had obligations to fulfill in Israel.

When I was nine, my family had a clothing business in Tel Aviv; my father was the designer and my mother sewed. I remember as a young boy how much I enjoyed playing with the sewing machines. I was curious to know how everything worked. I could take anything apart and put it back together. It always gave me a thrill, a wonderful sense of accomplishment. But then my family moved to Jerusalem and my father went into business with my oldest brother, Joseph, selling detergent to supermarkets and hotels.

After I matriculated in the United States, I returned to Jerusalem and went to work in the family business as a bookkeeper. I hated it, so I switched to marketing and then to management. I was using the knowledge I had gained at Lawrence, but there was nothing in the detergent business to engage my curiosity, no outlet for my creative tinkering. My heart was not in it. I needed something more.

I held out for seven years until I met and married a beautiful Israeli-born makeup artist named Orly. That's when I decided it was time to make a change. Time to go back to America.

It was December 31, 1974, when Orly and I arrived in Los Angeles just in time to welcome the New Year.

We moved west because Orly didn't like Michigan's frigid winters. She was used to Israel's desert climate. I wasn't sure what I was going to do in Los Angeles, but I did like the sunny days, the beaches, and the pioneering spirit of the city that would become our home. I thought perhaps I would be a real estate developer like my brother, but then I happened upon the idea of opening a perfumery.

All over Europe, there were small, cozy corner shops where women bought perfumes and various skin care products. Perfumeries were born from the lack of department stores in Europe, and their appeal rested largely on the fact that they provided personal service to their customers. It was this aspect that appealed to me—the personal touch, the opportunity to create one-on-one relationships with customers and I thought I could replicate this model in California.

The only problem was that by the 1970s, department stores had become an iconic part of the American consumer landscape and, as such, vendors of women's beauty products would only sell to the major retail chains like Saks Fifth Avenue and Macy's, effectively destroying the development and proliferation of the small, intimate corner perfumery that was so popular in Europe.

As luck would have it, a mutual friend introduced me to Jack Sperling, who owned a small beauty supply shop and warehouse in Van Nuys, California.

In the 1970s, beauty supply stores like Jack's sold nearly exclusively to professionals: hairdressers, manicurists, and the like. I wasn't entirely sure my future lay in women's beauty products, but I knew that I liked business.

Perhaps that's an understatement.

I love business—the challenge of it, the creativity that it takes to succeed. I believe this is why so many of us are drawn to the world of business.

It's January 1975. Jack Sperling and I are sitting in his warehouse surrounded by bottles of shampoo and hair conditioner, some of which he purchased at a ridiculously discounted price from a manufacturer in Los Angeles whose plant was gutted by fire.

An idea has been clanking around in my head. I don't know if Jack will go for it, but I've never been one to run from risk, so I take a deep breath and begin.

"I want to learn about your business," I say. "The way I figure it, I can work for you for five years and learn everything there is to know about the business and then maybe open a store that is similar to yours. But I have another proposition."

Jack sits, fingers laced beneath his chin, a look of bemusement on his face.

I can tell he doesn't exactly know what to make of me, what with my thick Israeli accent and brashness.

"Go on," he says.

"I want to work for you for ninety days. For free. In fact, I'll pay you to teach me the business. After ninety days, help me open a beauty supply store ten miles from here so I won't be in competition with you."

My words hang in the space between us. Jack is quiet, contemplative. "That's a very strange proposition," he says, finally. "Let me think about it."

I don't know exactly what possessed me to make such a proposition. At the time it sounded good, reasonable even. I'd already spent three years at university and several years working in the family business. Now I was chomping at the bit to start my own business. I didn't want to lose any more time. What could I learn from him in five years that I couldn't learn from him in ninety days?

I would come to appreciate over time that Jack Sperling is an out-of-the-box thinker like me. He accepted my proposition to the tune of ninety days and $2,500, which, in 1975, was quite a lot of money.

Now, thirty days in, I'm not so sure about this. My wife, Orly, is five months pregnant with our first child Ran and I'm spending each day counseling women about the technicalities of hair color or hand lotion or lipstick, things about which I have very little knowledge and even less interest.

Beauty supply stores are not like your neighborhood drug store where a clerk points you to the shampoo aisle but can't begin to advise you on which shampoo is right for your hair type. In beauty supply, the customer expects you to explain how to use each product in order to avoid going to an expensive salon and they expect you to be upbeat and positive, to demonstrate confidence that you know exactly what they need.

I decide that my wife Orly would be a lot better at this and might even enjoy it. After all, she is a trained makeup artist with an intimate knowledge of makeup and hair styling. When I suggest it to her, she shakes her head. "I'm going to take care of our children," she says. "You run the business."

With Jack's offer to reimburse me the entire $2,500 I've already paid him if I don't end up liking the business, I figure I don't really have anything to lose except another sixty days.

So, I grit my teeth, take Jack's advice, and dig in.

Jack Sperling and Jeff at the grand opening of
Jeff Pink's Beauty Supply, 1975.

Orly Pink, 1977.

Jeff Pink at his first professional
beauty show (BBSI) Las Vegas, 1979.

Jeff and Orly Pink, 1982.

2

ON MY WAY TO SOMEWHERE

It's April 1, 1975. The mid-spring sun is warm and I'm about to cut the ribbon on the Jeff Pink's Beauty Supply store squeezed between a See's Candy store and a manicurist shop located in a little strip mall in the San Fernando Valley of Los Angeles. Tarzana, to be exact. It's been less than three months since Jack and I had that crucial conversation about sticking with it, and today everything we discussed is coming true.

Standing in the April sunshine, right by my side, are the two people I've learned to count on most: my wife Orly, grinning from ear to ear and looking beautiful in a white linen maternity dress, and Jack Sperling, whose wise day-to-day counsel has kept me going in the right direction.

I know Jack is feeling the same pride I am. He looks up at the newly-minted sign across the front window. "So, how does it feel?" I can only nod and smile. For once, I, who love to talk, am speechless. I'm brimming with joy and gratitude. I am, as they say in Yiddish, "kvelling."

It may not seem like much, this little out-of-the-way shop in a remote location on the western edge of San Fernando Valley, but it's mine. The store and inventory have cost me my entire savings, $12,000, and it was worth every penny. My dream of creating something of my own is here right before my eyes. I'm on my way to becoming an entrepreneur, the epitome of the American dream. Now all I have to do is not screw it up.

It hasn't escaped me that there is a certain brazenness to launching a new business on April Fool's Day. But that's who I am. Like they say, "Fools rush in where angels fear to tread."

My job now is to figure out how I'm going to thrive in this world of shampoo, hair spray, styling mousse, makeup and nail polish. I know—after working with Jack Sperling—that if I'm going be successful, I need to learn everything I can about the beauty supply business starting with every product in the store.

I read whatever I can get my hands on about the beauty industry: trade publications, product manuals, and fashion magazines. I pay attention when new products come on the market and learn about their ingredients, how to use them, and what they are intended to do.

While I'm educating myself, I blanket Tarzana and surrounding neighborhoods with store flyers and discount coupons. The return is less than impressive. No matter how much I keep my nose to the grindstone, business remains sluggish.

Two months after we open the store, our first son Ran is born, and life takes on a whole new meaning. It's no longer just Orly and me. Now we're a family.

"Jeff, it's not just about knowing the products." Orly is in the kitchen, stirring a pot with one hand and cradling the baby with the other. "You have to understand the customers."

I listen to Orly because she's smart. She gives me good advice. She's my touchstone, my biggest supporter in everything I do. "What do you mean?" Orly stops stirring and points the wooden spoon at me. "Jeff, when a woman comes into a beauty supply store, she's not just looking for shampoo…she's looking for magic! Something that makes her feel beautiful."

I nod in agreement. "Sure, that's why they call it the beauty business."

She laughs. "Of course, but the beauty business is not just about selling product. It's about connecting with your customers and helping them feel good about themselves. Maybe that shampoo you're selling her isn't the magic potion that will turn her stringy hair into a glossy mane, but if she likes working with you, she'll come back."

She doesn't say another word, just goes back to stirring the pot. She's made her point.

I think about this a lot and realize what I love most about business is the marketing, the management, the creative aspects. The retail part—dealing with inventory, chatting with customers—doesn't really excite me. But in business you're always learning and sometimes what you must learn is how to do the thing you like the least—in my case, engaging with the customer.

I know I have a genuine interest in people, so I decide that when I talk to the customers, I'll make it more about them and not all about selling the product.

This approach—focusing on the customer rather than just pushing a product—has a noticeable effect. More than once a customer says, "Jeff, I love talking to you…and that accent…it's so charming. And by the way, why don't you give me two bottles of that shampoo? Might as well have an extra one in case I run out." This is a skill I didn't learn at Lawrence Tech.

While getting Jeff Pink's Beauty Supply off the ground, I've been studying the giants of the beauty world like Revlon and L'Oréal. I know that at this stage of my career it would be foolish to try to go head-to-head with them by introducing a product to the marketplace because they have huge name recognition and distribution channels that a guy like me doesn't have at his disposal—not yet anyway, but I think about it. What I need is to carve out my own niche. I'm not exactly sure what that is, but I know it's out there waiting for me. "Find the need," I keep telling myself. But it's Jack Sperling's advice that once again rings true. "Keep your eyes and ears open and the need will find you."

Patience is not my strong suit. I've never been very good at just waiting around for things to happen, so I decide to get out into the world going door-to-door the old-fashioned way, like the Fuller Brush man.

I target every hair salon in the San Fernando Valley from Studio City to Woodland Hills and meet in-person with the owners, the managers and the stylists. I'm interested in their comments and their ideas and I let them know that whatever they need, Jeff Pink's Beauty Supply will go the extra mile to get it for them. Once again, the personal touch pays off.

The hair stylists begin to know me by name. They have questions, which I'm able to answer because I've done my homework. They wait to place their orders with me because they like the personal attention I give them…and yes, many of them also like my "interesting accent."

But it's the manicurists, who occupy the least important space at the back of the salons, who brighten up the most when I come by to say hello. They're so grateful that someone cares enough to ask them about their work that they open up to me about what they need, what would make their jobs more rewarding, not just financially but also artistically. Most of them are young, beautiful women…so it's not such a difficult task to talk to them.

I start to get a bigger picture of the world that I'm a part of and I sense that somewhere in that world is a void that I am destined to fill.

Jack Sperling and I become very close friends. After he helps me open my own store, Jack and I start buying products together from the different major manufacturers and distribution companies. I can't meet their minimum order requirements on my own, but if I bundle my orders with his, it's easy, and we're able to negotiate favorable prices. I really appreciate his help, and as we collaborate, our friendship is cemented.

Then after about a year he calls me up one day and says "Jeff, we can't buy together anymore. "

I question him, "Why, Jack? I'm still a small company."

"Jeff, you're going to have to learn to do it for yourself, and one day, you're going to thank me for it."

Slowly I learn to buy directly from suppliers on my own. It's trial and error and it takes courage for me to start purchasing in larger amounts. But I do it, and to my surprise, I'm able to sell what I buy. As time goes on, I learn how to buy a little bit more or a little bit less, until I get the feel for how to manage my inventory. Once again, Jack Sperling is right.

It's early September 1976 and the Los Angeles weather is changing from the unbearable heat of summer to the tolerable warmth of fall. Business begins to pick up and finally, for the first time, I'm able to make the rent on the store and pay the household bills without falling behind.

Still, there are nagging questions that keep plaguing me. "Why am I not moving forward? Why is it that all I'm doing is making the rich companies richer? Why am I not doing anything for myself?" It seems like I'm just standing still. Then an answer comes to me in a very unexpected way.

13

Who would guess that a pungent smell wafting from the back of the salon I'm visiting would change my life? "What's that?" I ask.

The manicurist looks up at me and raises her penciled eyebrows. "It's the smell of acrylic nails. They're the newest thing."

Her young customer proudly holds up her completed right hand, flashing a full set of perfectly formed nails. "Aren't they fantastic?" She wiggles the unfinished fingers of her left hand. "This is what my own nails look like." I can see why she wants better-looking nails. Her own are a mess.

"What is it you're doing there?" I ask. The manicurist glows with pride as if I'd asked her to explain the theory of relativity and she begins to instruct me on the complicated method of applying layers of acrylic onto the nail one by one until they harden into a thickness that can be filed and painted.

It's tedious and time-consuming to say nothing of the awful smell. But by the look on the young customer's face, I can see that the final result is exactly what she was hoping for.

As I drive home, I can't stop thinking, "Why are women willing to put themselves through this unpleasant and time-consuming procedure in order to have a decent set of nails? Aren't there any alternatives?"

Back at Jeff Pink's Beauty Supply, I examine every nail care product I have in stock. They all fall into the same three categories: base coat, topcoat, and color. None of them are targeted to do the job of creating what the manicurists are after—a product that can strengthen a woman's own nails, allowing them to grow.

I check nail care catalogues. Nothing! The closest thing I find is a product called "Juliette" that uses thin strips of paper applied with glue to cover and protect the nail. It's clumsy and unimaginative. I can see that what's needed is a simple formula, something that can be brushed on the nail that contains a strengthening element;

something easier for the manicurist to use or maybe even something a woman can use at home.

That night, when I lock the store, I feel like I've just discovered Atlantis. I've found a "need." Now all I have to do is figure out how to fulfill it. When I tell my wife, Orly, about my brainstorm, she raises her eyebrows and gives me one of those nods that says, "You might be on to something." Every great new venture needs a blessing and from the look on her face, I know I have mine.

When I call Abe Rosenbaum in New Jersey, he is already a legend in the nail polish industry—a creative genius who went from making paint for automobiles to discovering the formula for Revlon's high-quality nail colors.

"Why not go right to the top?" I ask myself. "The worst he can do is turn me down." He doesn't. Instead, he suggests I come to New York and meet him. I've got enough chutzpah, and I'm young enough that I jump at the chance to meet this *eminence gris*.

The lobby of the Sofitel Hotel, with its comfortable brown leather chairs and elegant patterned carpet feels like a safe haven, a place where my crazy new idea can be launched into the world and not get shot down.

At the appointed hour I spot Abe Rosenbaum. He's a smartly-dressed gentleman in his seventies. He walks with a slight shuffle leaning on a hand-carved cane that gives him an air of elegance. I wonder if we'll have much in common. Abe has already made his fortune a couple of times. He has nothing to prove. When I ask him why he wants to help someone like me who hasn't done anything yet, he says, "Jeff, I'm getting older. My work has been very satisfying. It's given me a good life. It's time for me to give something back."

We hit it off immediately. I quickly learn that Abe Rosenbaum still has a fertile, eager mind and enjoys a new challenge...just like me. When I tell him what I'm thinking about—a product to strengthen the nail that can be brushed on—his eyes light up.

I fly back to Los Angeles filled with eager anticipation. We both know it will take a lot of experimentation to come up with a nail strengthening product, but I suggest using nylon fibers in a base coat and Abe runs with the idea. Within a few weeks he has a test batch.

I give the nail strengthener to a number of manicurists and at first everything looks promising. But one problem keeps cropping up—the nylon fibers won't lie flat. They stick out in all directions and the manicurist has to apply three or four topcoats to make the nail surface smooth; then they can apply the polish. But it's too much work and is unsatisfactory.

It's back to the drawing board. Rather than changing the strengthener formula, we agree that some kind of filler has to go on the nail that has a powder in it. The question is "What kind of powder?"

While Abe is experimenting on the East Coast, I'm in the back room of the store with my own little lab trying different combinations: flour, baking soda, face powder. And then I hit on it. My son Ran is still in diapers, and while I was changing his diaper, the instruction I got from my wife to use talc baby powder before tightening the diaper turns out to reveal the perfect secret ingredient.

I quickly call Abe and he sounds a bit skeptical, but—with a laugh—he says he'll give it a try. Two days later, he gives me the news. We have a winner with two separate products that will do the trick—a Nail Strengthener and a Filler. And what's even more amazing is we discover that the filler can also be used to fill the ridges of a woman's nails to smooth them out, so the product has two uses and I name it Ridgefiller.

Abe sends me a five-gallon drum of his new filler and we hand fill 1,500 bottles, stuff them into padded envelopes along with the Romeo Strengthener and send them to beauty supply stores all over the country with a letter:

These are our new products to strengthen the nails—
the Romeo Strengthener and the Ridgefiller.
Give them to your secretary, give them to your wife,
give them to your girlfriend and let me know if they like them.
With the compliments of Jeff Pink

The response is incredible. Storeowners and manicurists go crazy for it. Three months later we're in the wholesale market with our kit, which we call "Romeo," designed, of course, to compete head to head with the clumsy paper and glue product, "Juliette."

Jeff Pink's Beauty Supply isn't just a store anymore; it's a manufacturing company with two products! At last, I'm on my way to somewhere!

Romeo—first nail strengthener
on the market.

Ridgefiller—first primer basecoat
on the market.

The Romeo Kit—a combination of Romeo and Ridgefiller.

18

3

BABY STEPS

The first big order we receive is from a guy in New Orleans, Lenny Goldberg. He calls me up and says, "Jeff, you don't know me, but I have two beauty supply stores. I like your product. I want to order a large quantity."

That's the good news. The bad news is I didn't have large quantities. We are hand-filling the bottles and assembling the packages one item at a time in the back room of the store. Then, Lenny Goldberg says, "Jeff, this is going to be really big. I think you need a master distributor."

Making the right move at the right time can make all the difference. Wait too long…think too much…carefully consider all the pros and cons…and the golden opportunity can slip right by you. "Go with your gut," has always worked for me and I knew Lenny Goldberg was right. It was time to step up my game and take a chance on the Romeo Kit.

I rent a 650-square-foot space in Tarzana on Reseda Boulevard. It's an empty shell that I'll have to equip, but I'm excited and feel that this is the beginning of a new adventure.

I name the company ORLY, in honor of my wife, and hire a small staff: an all-around assistant, Barbara Radin, and a head of shipping and assembly, Ron Pelleg. We sign a contract with a master distribution company, Spilo, and just like that ORLY is up and running.

We're still a little hands-on outfit, with the store personnel handling our retail customers while I concentrate on the professional salon market of manicurists and hair stylists. I continue making my personal appearances at salons, but now Ron Pelleg is handling all the follow-up deliveries. It frees me to come up with some new ideas.

"Monday Night Manicures" is a notion that struck me when I was thinking about how to promote the Romeo Kit and other products from my beauty supply store that I still owned. From watching the manicurists, I saw that when something new came on the market and they didn't know how to use it they would hesitate. They needed a little help, a little confidence building. I decide to do a workshop where manicurists could learn about new products.

I don't want it to be just a sales pitch for the Romeo Kit, so I call the company that makes the acrylic nails—which I carry in my store—and invite them to come to our special night where they can train manicurists on how to use their product. They are more than happy to send an "educator" because it means more sales for them.

Monday is the traditional day that salons are closed so I rent a conference room in a local hotel and invite a group of manicurists. They listen eagerly to the lecture and demonstration and ask a lot of questions.

At the end I take over and show them all the products on the market that are similar to acrylics including our Romeo Kit. When the evening is over the women crowd around me all excited, "Jeff, this was fantastic. Now I know how to use these products and can recommend them to my clients with complete confidence as the way to make the nails stronger and longer naturally."

They all nod in agreement. "And that Romeo Kit. It's so fast. I can do three or four of those in the time it takes to do one set of acrylic nails. That's a whole lot more money in my pocket!"

That's exactly what I want to hear. It was a win/win situation for everyone. Once again, it was a matter of discovering a "need" and filling it. Slowly but surely, the Romeo Kit began finding its way into the world of nail care products.

Life is not without its ups and downs and often the greatest lessons are learned from the biggest mistakes. Mine cost me a bundle. Once the Romeo Kit had gained a foothold in the beauty industry, I decided that it was time to register the name of my company, ORLY.

I had been thinking about doing it for a while, but we were so involved in developing and marketing the Romeo Kit that I kept putting it off. I figured, "Who but me is going to name their company ORLY?" Some guy in Queens! That's who.

When I learn that the name has already been registered, I make a trip to New York to meet with the trademark owner who has a small corner store in Queens. I have a purchase agreement in my pocket prepared by my attorney in the event that we can strike a deal. The owner is a wiry little guy with a nervous tic and he wants $15,000 for the name.

"Are you crazy? That's outrageous! I'm not willing to pay that. I'll change the name of my company," I say. There's a long pause. He flicks the ash from his cigarette onto the linoleum floor. "So, what are you willing to pay for it?" We finally settle on $5,000. But he has some very strange terms.

"I want the money delivered in cash."

My first thought is, "Cash?" That means he wants the transaction to be off the books. I go back to my hotel with an uneasy feeling and contact my bank in L.A. I ask them to wire the funds to a bank next to my hotel.

The following day, I visit the bank and introduce myself to the branch manager. I tell him that I am expecting to have a $5,000 wire transfer any time today and I need the money that afternoon. He looks at me suspiciously, "We close at three o'clock. You can wait here and if it comes in, I'll give you the cash."

Then I hear him speaking to someone on the phone in Italian and my paranoia really kicks in. I'm thinking to myself, "He'll give me the cash and then when I leave the bank, he'll have one of his guys jump me!" I think I've seen too many gangster movies. I'm sweating. I decide I need protection.

Immediately I call Danny Korn, my friend from Jerusalem who now lives in New York, and ask him to meet me at the bank. "I don't know that anything is going to happen, but I'd feel a lot safer if you waited for me outside the bank." He answers, "Sure, anything for you, Jeff."

Time goes by and I'm waiting for the money. It's almost three o'clock. I'm concerned that I might leave the bank empty-handed. Luckily a minute before three o'clock, the manager gives me a voucher and I go to the cashier and ask for the money. The cashier tells me, "I'm sorry to tell you, Mr. Pink, I don't have large bills. I'll have to give you the cash in twenty-dollar bills." I told him, "I don't care…I'll take it in one-dollar bills if I have to." He hands me a large envelope stuffed with bills. In New York City, they'll rob you for $100. With this much money, I'll probably be cut to pieces.

It's the dead of winter and Danny arrives by taxi wearing a heavy coat and Russian fur hat and takes up a post outside the front door of the bank, which has just closed. Now the bank manager gets suspicious. He says to me, "There's a strange guy outside. Are you waiting for someone?"

"You talking about the guy with the Russian hat? He's my friend. You've got nothing to worry about." Then I laugh. "I know he looks a bit suspicious, but trust me, he's a good guy."

Danny and I jump into a taxi. Much to my relief, the Queens handoff goes without a hitch. Finally, with a little bit of cloak and dagger, the name ORLY is mine.

I've learned an important lesson about how easy it is for something critical to be overlooked, especially when everyone is focused on launching a new product and a new company. I promise myself that from then on, I'll be diligent about paying attention to the details that can make or break a business. I become obsessive about taking care of legal matters because I know in the long run it will save me a lot of money.

Back in Los Angeles, I settle into a daily routine: checking on the beauty supply store, making sure everything is running smoothly at ORLY's warehouse, and calling on my customers. Things are going well, business is picking up, and my wife is pregnant with our second child, Tal, which is putting more pressure on me to succeed.

I'm confident that I will, but I know that I need to put one foot in front of the other—I can't run before I can walk. And from watching my son, Ran, learn how to take his first steps, I know that you fall down many times before you finally learn how to confidently put one foot in front of the other.

I have a vision for the future of ORLY—to be a leader in the beauty industry—but I don't think it's any one product that's going to make it happen. I believe that it's the cumulative effect of every product that we develop that will get us there. I know instinctively that it's not all about just making money. I want to enjoy the ride and every time I introduce a new product into the market— something that has never been there before—I feel a sense of pride. It's like bringing a child into the world and carefully nurturing it. I accept that it will take time; as I'm becoming more mature, I'm learning the virtue of patience, even if I don't always exhibit the trait all the time.

4

IT'S ONLY NATURAL

The movie studios were important customers of my beauty supply business. I enjoyed working with the heads of the makeup and hair departments. I feel very comfortable in that atmosphere because, as I discover, my marketing and promotion efforts have a lot in common with the movie business: they both require a sense of showmanship and a desire to engage and inspire others. I like the people I'm working with because they are all top professionals at the studios.

One day, I'm making my usual rounds of the studios, schmoozing with the head makeup artist at Paramount Pictures, when a director comes flying in with that "time-is-money look" in his eyes. "Where the hell is she? We've been ready for twenty minutes!"

The makeup artist shakes her head, "Her nail polish isn't dry. She needs another ten minutes."

The director turns on me as if it's my fault.

"This is what I go through at least three times a day. Every time she changes her wardrobe, she changes her nail color to match. I've got an entire crew standing around waiting for polish to dry! You know how much that costs? You people need to come up with a nail polish color that will go with everything the actress is wearing during the shoot."

With that, the director storms out the door like a tornado, leaving the makeup artist stammering to apologize to me for his rude behavior. But all I hear are his last words "…you need to come up with a nail polish color that will go with everything."

"Keep your eyes and ears open, Jeff…it will come to you!" Once again, Jack Sperling's wisdom reverberates in my head. This director has unknowingly challenged me, started my creative juices flowing and dropped a gem in my lap.

"A color that will go with everything." What could that be? I know it's not enough just to do a simple neutral color…this is Hollywood…it needs some glitz, some glamour. Something that will make it stand out, catch your eye, and, of course, go with everything.

At my beauty supply store, I rummage through all the products in the nail line and come across a white pencil—one of the least-used items in the manicurist's kit. Sometimes, when the manicurist is cleaning under the nails and can't remove every bit of discoloration, she'll draw under the nail with the white pencil. It makes the nail look perfectly clean and ready to be polished, or the nails can be buffed and worn naturally without nail polish. Something about that white pencil captures my attention and my mind starts going a mile a minute.

Who knows where creative ideas come from or how they lead us from one thing to another? Just at that moment, I literally see a set of beautifully polished nails in a soft neutral color with sparkling white tips. I know in an instant this is going to be my next big thing. I call Abe Rosenbaum in New Jersey and tell him I want him to make me a gallon of white nail polish. I can hear on the other end of the phone that he's laughing. "Jeff, you're crazy. No woman is going to wear white nail polish."

"Abe, this is something special; it's for the movies." You can get away with a lot when you say something is for the movies. Everyone expects that movie people want crazy things. A week later, Abe delivers a gallon of white polish. It's very bright and I have to make sure that the balance between the natural nail color and the white tip is just right.

I do my usual testing to find the correct formula. In what order do we paint it on? White tip first? Neutral color first? What's the right neutral color to soften the brightness of the white? How big should the white tip be in relation to the neutral portion of the nail?

It's a lot of trial and error, but when I have exactly the look I envisioned, I go back to the studio and show the director what I've come up with: a glamorous looking neutral manicure that will go with any costume, whatever the color. The director is so impressed he tells me I deserve an Oscar!

"Jeff, you don't know how much money you just saved us." He gathers everyone in the makeup and wardrobe departments and tells them that from now on this is what he wants them to use on the actresses' nails. The word starts spreading. Hollywood is a very small community and before long all the studios have adopted the look.

I immediately develop the packaging for the "Natural Nail Look" and aggressively market it in a single kit, selling it not only to the movie studios but also to beauty supply distributors nationwide.

The white-tipped nails start appearing in movies and on television. The actresses love it and the studios love it, but it's not an overnight sensation. This is 1977, and as much as Hollywood and New York like the new manicure, it's slow to take off in Middle America. To our disappointment, our small staff of three have to deal with an exceptional amount of returns, which is followed by a lot of in-house discussion about changing our focus…not putting so much emphasis on "The Natural Nail Look."

It's times like these when you need to defend your creation against the naysayers. Anytime you introduce a new product to the market, it will meet resistance from certain customers who are closed-minded and cannot see the advantages of what you have created. It takes a kind of blind faith to keep going. Fortunately, that's what I have. It may take time for people to accept it, but I know that sooner or later "The Natural Nail Look" will take off.

In the meantime, a new problem crops up that will once again change the direction of Jeff Pink's Beauty Supply. One of my nail polish suppliers is a small company called FINGERPAINTS. It's a nice product, it sells well at the store, but the owner of the company, Gail Freeman, is operating on a close margin and is strapped for cash. I agree to pay her every two weeks, rather than every thirty days to help her out.

Like clockwork, she delivers my orders and picks up her check every other Friday. Before long, Jeff Pink's Beauty Supply is her biggest customer.

One week when I'm out of town, Gail comes into the store and my assistant tells her that I'll be gone for another week. Can she wait until then to get paid? Gail becomes agitated and refuses. "I'm not leaving any more product until I get paid." She storms out.

Life is too short to deal with this kind of unpleasantness. When I return, I call Gail and politely ask her to please come pick up her remaining merchandise from my store, which she does. I give her a check for the balance I owe her and it's goodbye FINGERPAINTS.

It's not a happy ending but it turns me in a new direction. I decide it's time to start my own brand of nail polish.

All it takes is a call to the venerable Abe Rosenbaum who, when he hears what I want to do, is all for it. Abe has become more than a business associate; he's become my mentor. He gives me advice and watches out for my well-being. Abe wants me to succeed. I'm lucky to have Abe in my corner. Everyone should be so fortunate.

We select twenty-four colors to start our line of nail polishes, and bingo, ORLY is a nail polish manufacturer. We're still filling bottles by hand at the warehouse and I hire more workers to keep up with the orders. That's when we realize that the name ORLY is receiving market recognition. By the end of 1977, The Romeo Kit and the ORLY nail polish line are doing so well that we're running out of space in our 650-square-foot warehouse. It's time to expand. We move to a 5,000-square-foot warehouse in Chatsworth, which is about thirty minutes away from the Tarzana store. It may seem like a quantum leap, but I am confident that we'll eventually need the additional capacity because I have lots of ideas for ORLY products and I'm confident that the market for our existing product will continue to grow.

I'm not sure where this confidence comes from, but it may be a combination of having proven to myself that I could do what I set out to do, combined with blind faith that the future would somehow take care of itself if I just kept putting my *all* into the business.

In 1978, out of the blue, a guy named Stanley Wild calls me and says, "You don't know me, Mr. Pink, but I'm your new representative in the Northeast." I've never heard of him, but I like his chutzpah. We talk for a few minutes and he informs me that he has ten salespeople who work on commission for him and that he really knows the northeast market and thinks that ORLY could do very well there.

The U.S. professional nail products market is divided into five territories: the Northeast, which is New York and all the surrounding states; the Southeast, which is Florida and all the states around it; the Midwest, that's Michigan, Illinois etc.; the Southwest, which is Texas and those surrounding states; and the West Coast, which covers California, Oregon, Nevada and other surrounding states.

I didn't have anyone representing ORLY in the Northeast so I said, "You know what. You're hired." Stanley did an incredible job, and sales in the Northeast went from zero to amazing in a short period of time.

At the same time, the Natural Nail Look is not performing as I had hoped. Sales continue to be sluggish. And then something unexpected happens. In early 1978, I'm on the phone with a friend who's involved with runway shows in Paris. We enjoy talking about how things are going in our work. I tell him about my latest creation, The Natural Nail Look, and all the attention it's been getting at the movie studios.

He says, "You ought to bring it to Paris for Fashion Week." That sounds like a great idea. I ask him if he can help connect me with someone who's involved with the runway shows.

A few days later he's come up with the name of a woman who is in charge of the hair and makeup for the models. That's what friends are for. He's already talked to her about my product and she's interested. This is very good news. I fly to Paris with a supply of kits.

With my friend acting as my interpreter, I demonstrate the Natural Nail Look for the Fashion Week staff, and to my delight,

30

the response is enthusiastic. The manicurists appreciate the benefits of the Natural Nail Look: the designers don't have to worry about whether the polish will clash with the fashions and the models love the look and ease of it.

It's not a done deal yet because we still need the approval of several designers. I'm confident they will like it and by the next day it's confirmed—some models in the Paris Fashion Week will be wearing ORLY's Natural Nail Look.

The opening night is a glamorous black-tie affair. I'm seated in the front row alongside the rich and famous: movie stars, wealthy socialites, and all the top names in the fashion world. They're all intensely focused on the designer clothes, but all I can see is the nail polish. And it is beautiful.

The whole evening is a parade of long-legged beauties, strutting and posing, and all wearing the Natural Nail Look. Every hand that is placed on a hip or raised to emphasize a feature of the garment, shines with my creation. The idea that the Natural Nail Look, a product that I created for Hollywood, is now gaining international attention makes me very proud.

I fly back to Los Angeles and in the middle of telling my wife Orly how great the Natural Nails looked on the models, an idea strikes me...I want to change the name from The Natural Nail Look to The French Manicure. Orly gives me "that nodding look" and I know I'm on the right track.

Americans love what's foreign and exotic (look how they go on about my accent!). The name—French Manicure—suggests that our product has something to do with a country known for its glamour, its fashion sense, its romance, its *je ne sais quoi*. So what could be better than to communicate these ideas in a name? The next day, I meet with the ORLY graphic design team and tell them I want to completely change the look of the kit based on the name

The French Manicure. I hire Richard Kline, a wonderful graphic artist, to design the packaging and create a poster for The French Manicure.

Richard comes up with an image of a French Manicured hand and a single dewy-fresh strawberry. It's an abstract concept with no direct reference to the product, but its simplicity and visual elegance capture the eye and soon the poster becomes iconic and it is hanging in nail salons all over the country.

Serendipitously, Barbra Streisand appears on the *Tonight Show with Johnny Carson* wearing The French Manicure on her long, acrylic nails and Johnny is so fascinated that he wants to know everything about this "new manicure." And if that wasn't enough, a few weeks later, Cher appears on the show, and once again Johnny makes a big deal about her French Manicure. It's the kind of publicity money can't buy. And we didn't!

Despite all this free publicity, we're still not an overnight sensation. We see an uptick in sales, but it's 1979 and at that time new products could take up to five years to establish themselves in the marketplace. So I take it all in stride.

Still, a lot of women start to notice the actresses in movies and on TV wearing The French Manicure, which generates positive word of mouth. It's not a big seller yet, but across the country, women begin asking for The French Manicure. I believe in my product and anticipate there will be an increasing demand for it. I order additional inventory and that's when I realize we're running out of warehouse space. It's time to take another giant leap.

The French Manicure individual bottles.

The French Manicure Kit.

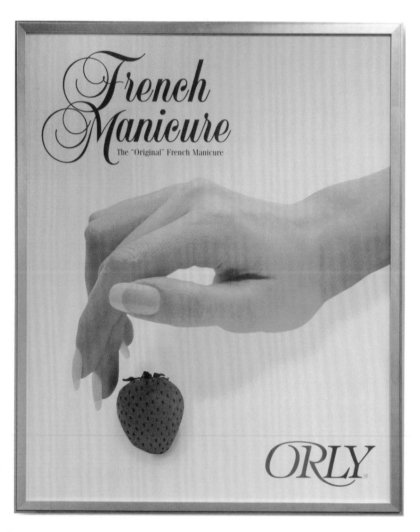

The French Manicure vintage poster.

5

LEARNING ON THE JOB

Jeff Pink's Beauty Supply store was a great place to launch my career in the beauty products industry, but now I'm doing what I truly love, which is coming up with new products and working with the professionals in the movie studios and the salons. After four years in business, it's time to sell the store and focus all my energy on building ORLY into a nail products powerhouse.

It's 1979. ORLY has about ten or fifteen employees. I want to promote my personal assistant Barbara Radin to a sales position, so I start looking for a new personal assistant.

Irene Wooley is from New York and when she applies for the job, as far as I can tell, she's a very mature person which I believe will be beneficial to me. I ask her age (in 1979, you're allowed to ask.). She says, "Jeff, I'm not going to tell you my age because you might not hire me." I say, "As far as I'm concerned, you're already hired. I just want to know for myself." She says she's forty-nine. I say, "Good, you're my new assistant." I have an instinct about hiring women and how valuable their input can be, especially for a company like ORLY, whose products are, for the most part, directed at a female customer base.

Neither of us knew at the time that this relationship would last for eighteen years, but Irene was a perfect choice and wore many hats. Not only was she my assistant, she did the payroll and the bookkeeping until we were able to afford full-time staff for those positions. Irene turned out to be a real asset to ORLY and I'm proud to have hired her.

Hiring new people takes some expertise and I developed a few skills that turned out to be very helpful. One of them, I think I was born with: I can analyze people quite well. I can tell after sitting down with someone for ten or fifteen minutes if I'm going to like working with them.

I can see from their manners, their behavior, and their responses to my questions if they are a good fit for the company and if they agree with the way I run the company. I don't like to hire people who go from one job to another every year. I want people who are steady, who stay with a job for a substantial length of time. I review their résumé to make sure that they aren't job hopping and if they have moved around, why this is so. Sometimes there are valid reasons for staying in a position for a year or less, but that's usually not the case. I want to hire people who intend to make a long-term commitment to ORLY.

I also have a bias against hiring people who travel great distances to get to work. A long commute can be enervating and frustrating and can affect a person's disposition and energy. If they live more than an hour away, by the time they get here, they're tired. When they go home, they're tired. Eventually, it makes for an unhappy employee. Ideally, I prefer that my employees live no more than thirty or forty minutes away at the most.

I admit that there are many aspects of running a company that I may not know even to this day. But at least I know that there are things I don't know, and if that's the case, I find people who do. In assessing my strengths and weaknesses, on the plus side of the ledger, I consider myself realistic about myself. I know what I can do and what I can't. When I started ORLY, I was really struggling, wondering: "What do I do first? What should my priorities be? How do I build the company in such a way that I'll not only be able to service my customers but also develop new products?"

When you work for one of the big companies in corporate America, there is a system in place and a chain of command. A structure of what you do first and how you go from here to there. I didn't have that. I didn't come from that background. I had worked in my family's business in Israel and studied Industrial Management at Lawrence. I didn't have an MBA, so I recognized that if I was committed to growing ORLY, I'd have to acquire practical knowledge about running and growing a business as I went along. I knew that I needed someone with management and administrative skills, but the company was too small to hire someone full-time to fulfill these functions. What I could do was work with a consultant—someone I could hire on a freelance basis to train me.

I asked a few business associates if they knew someone they could recommend, and I was given the name Rick Niemrow, who owned a very successful drugstore on the corner of Santa Monica Boulevard and Beverly Glen in Los Angeles. I called him, and he agreed to come meet with me.

A few days later, Niemrow shows up at my office, takes one look around and says, "Can I look at your desk?" It's a strange request, but I say, "Sure." My desk is cluttered with papers, letters, order forms, some sample bottles of polish, a nail color chart, and the usual flyers and advertisements that come in the mail every day.

"Just tell me about every piece of paper on your desk and why it's there."

37

So I start to explain, "This one is a bill, this one is an order, this is a promotional flyer…"

Niemrow stops me, "You're the head of the company. You shouldn't be handling all this. All of this should go to other people."

Then he teaches me one of the most important lessons I'll ever learn. "If you're handling a paper two or three times, there's something wrong. You should be handling each piece of paper once…" He lets that idea sink in before he continues, "…and then it should be filed or go to somebody else to handle or go in the trash."

It seems like such a simple idea, but it completely revolutionizes the way I think. After he leaves, I go through ever paper and apply his lesson. I create files, I delegate some of the paperwork to my assistants, and a lot goes in the trash.

The next day when Niemrow returns, my desk is clean and free of clutter. A deep sense of satisfaction comes over me. I have taken control of something I didn't even recognize as a problem to begin with.

Over subsequent meetings, Niemrow teaches me how to successfully manage a business; how I, as the owner, need to build a structure not only for myself but also for my employees so that we all have a clear idea of how things should run. The lessons I learn from Rick Niemrow are so important they become part of my DNA and I feel ready to take on the challenges we will inevitably face as ORLY continues to grow.

Our next big move is to expand the warehouse in Chatsworth by an additional 5,000 square feet and automate our production. There's a beautiful piece of machinery designed just for our needs. It's made in Italy and costs a good chunk of change. But there's no doubt in my mind that it will quadruple our manufacturing capacity. It's a big investment, but in 1983, I place an order for one machine.

It takes almost a year for the machine to be built to our specifications. The day the machine arrives, ORLY is buzzing with excitement. We all watch as the components are unpacked and assembled. I still love seeing how things are put together and for me, it's like watching the unveiling of an incredible artifact.

A representative from the company is there to explain the complex moving parts: "…the filing piston, the brush loader, the feeder unit, the cap inserter…" As he drones on, my mind goes back to my childhood fascination with the simple working of my mother's sewing machine in Israel. I look at this beautiful piece of machinery and think about how far I've come. I'm overwhelmed with a sense of pride and satisfaction.

The machine is wired up, the whirr of the motor starts, and the mechanical song and dance begins: a tinkling of regimented bottles as each one moves obediently into an assigned space, the gurgling of the polish sliding through the tubes in a measured stream, the robotic whirling of smooth metal parts rising and falling as they attend to their specific functions, and finally, the emergence of the finished product—the first machine-made bottle of red ORLY nail polish. When it comes off the conveyor belt the room explodes in applause and laughter. Someone breaks out a bottle of champagne and proposes a toast.

"To Jeff, to ORLY, and to the Machine."

Barbara Radin, my long-time assistant, hands me the first bottle of polish off the assembly line.

"This is for you, Jeff, as a reminder of this wonderful day."

I take the bottle gratefully, but I need no reminder. It's a day I will never forget.

We've all heard the term "marketing genius." I am not sure how to define it, but I know it when I see it or hear it. Perhaps it's a way to capture your customers' desires and to motivate those desires into buying your product.

For example, in the beauty industry the slogan, "Only your hairdresser knows for sure," was sheer marketing genius; women wanted the natural look when coloring their hair. They didn't want to look as if their color came out of a bottle. Or the ubiquitous "Because you're worth it!"—a phrase that tapped into a woman's belief in herself, that she was worth spending an extra few dollars on herself because she's worked hard for it and deserves it.

Whether changing the name to The French Manicure from the Natural Nail Look is "genius" or just "good marketing" (which is often enough to move product off the shelves and into a customer's hands) the product was suddenly a best seller and ORLY was becoming so successful that once again, after having had such a positive experience with Rick Niemrow in 1980 that I decide to hire another consultant. This time it will be someone who can teach me about product distribution and servicing customers.

I learn about a company called Mercury Distribution, run by two brothers, Mike and Rick Nave, and their father, Eddie Nave, who is semi-retired. I'm still working with my master distributor Spilo, but now that we're becoming more established, I want to try doing my own distribution.

Rick Nave knows all about distribution. He teaches me the ins and outs of the distribution and shipping business, and in a short time, I no longer work exclusively with one master distributor; I'm working with hundreds of distributors throughout the country. I supply directly to them and what's even better, I avoid having to pay the 25% fee that Spilo charges as a middleman.

Implementing the advice of the Mercury consultants, sales of ORLY products increase dramatically and we are ready for another change. We expand our space in Chatsworth from 10,000 square feet to 20,000 square feet, allowing us to comfortably house our burgeoning operation under one roof.

One day, my wife Orly tells me, "I met a very nice couple that moved here from Israel and they're having a hard time meeting their financial obligations. Do you think we can help them out?"

I think she's asking for a donation. "Sure, let's write them a check; whatever you think will help." Orly shakes her head. "No, Jeff, they don't want charity. They want to work."

I don't usually hire people as favors, but Orly convinces me that the wife, Zippi, can do any of the menial labor jobs on the factory floor and would be grateful for the work. "All right," I say. After all, how wrong can it go? I give her a job as a packer. It doesn't take much skill, but Zippi dives into the work with a passion.

To my surprise, I discover that Zippi is not only a great worker, she has a rare gift—one that every company needs. Zippi has a detailed, photographic memory. She can tell you when each of our products was manufactured, when it was shipped, and where it is stored. "Ask Zippi" becomes one of my standard answers to the multitude of questions I'm asked every day.

Zippi Gonsor becomes the walking encyclopedia of ORLY's inventory and what I learn is how valuable it can be to hire women; they bring an inherent work ethic and dedication that's hard to find. Zippi stays with the company for thirty-eight years and will forever be thought of as one of our most cherished employees. It's always a pleasant surprise when someone you've hired turns out to be much better than you imagined.

6

GROWING PAINS

By 1980, it's safe to say that ORLY is a major player in the beauty products world. After five years in business, we have become widely known for bringing new and innovative ideas to the market and our reputation for high quality has earned us a solid place in the industry.

On the home front, we learn that my wife, Orly, is pregnant again and we're expecting our third child. We're living in a very nice, three-bedroom home in Woodland Hills but with our growing family, it's beginning to feel cramped. Financially, we're doing well enough to start thinking about a bigger house.

We decide to build the house of our dreams: an English Tudor-style home with five bedrooms, beautiful grounds, a tennis court, a pool, a screening room, a state-of-the-art kitchen, and plenty of space for entertaining. This amazing house is a symbol of how far we've come. We finish it just in time for the birth of our third son, Dean, on January 22, 1981.

By now ORLY has reached a new level of success in the business world and I'm finally able to shift from part-time consultants to hiring full-time staff.

One of the first senior management hires is our vice president of sales, Frank Caldwell, who had worked at the cosmetics behemoth, Revlon. The first time we met, he said, "Jeff, your Ridgefiller was so popular I told Revlon they should copy it. They finally did, but it took them ten years." I liked him right away and my intuition about him proved to be correct as over the next five years he shaped ORLY's sales division into a dynamic, well-oiled machine.

Around this same time, I make another interesting acquaintance. It's 1982 and I'm on one of the constant business trips that keep me traveling from one end of the country to the other. On a flight home from New York, there are two women sitting next to me—a mother and her seventeen-year-old daughter. The daughter is tall and beautiful, and I instantly recognize her. She's the model and actress, Brooke Shields, who's featured everywhere these days in ads for Calvin Klein Jeans and Wella Balsam Shampoo. I introduce myself; we make small talk and settle in for the long flight. As the plane nears LAX the pilot comes on the loudspeaker to inform us that the airport is fogged in and we are being re-routed to Phoenix, Arizona.

The airline has arranged for buses to take us all to a hotel where we will wait in the lobby until the fog clears. There's a lot of moaning and groaning, but there's nothing we can do about it. We're captives of the weather and are all forced to go along with the plan, which, for me, turns out to have rather fortunate consequences.

When life gives you lemons…you know the rest. Brooke, her mother, and I spend a few very pleasurable hours together. We talk about all kinds of things. I tell them I'm in the nail care business, which they find very interesting and Brooke talks about the difficulty of juggling her career and her schoolwork. But mostly it's just an enjoyable conversation about life. Brooke is not only beautiful but also very bright.

While we sit in the hotel lobby, I become aware of how many people, not only the other passengers, but also hotel workers and guests, are pointing and staring at us. A few brave fans even dare to approach for an autograph, which Brooke graciously gives.

I get a brief taste of what it must be like for her to always be the center of attention and how in exchange for her career she has given up her right to privacy. Yet she handles it with great poise—quite a feat for someone so young.

The time passes quickly and soon we're all back on the bus heading for the airport. The diversion to Phoenix has given us a chance to get acquainted and as the plane touches down in Los Angeles, I promise that I will send them both some ORLY products. Brooke gives me her address and tells me not to forget. As if anyone could forget her!

The next day, I have a sampling of our nail care products and our polish colors shipped out with a note saying how enjoyable it was to meet the two of them. I don't expect to hear back, so a few weeks later when a large envelope arrives from Brooke it comes as a great surprise. Inside is a hand-written letter:

"Dear Mr. Pink, I'm sorry for the delay in writing but I have been really busy with work and school. I just wanted to thank you for all the beautiful nail polishes. I've tried so many of them already and love each one. Dear Mr. Pink, I hope you like the picture…love and kisses, Brooke."

I fish inside the envelope and pull out a beautiful photo of her inscribed to me and signed, *"Love and Happiness Always, Brooke."* I'm charmed by her response and it's not the last letter I will receive from her. We keep in touch over the years. I send nail polish. She sends photos.

Several years later, we meet again at a party. I'm not sure she'll remember me, and I say, "I'm Jeff, the man who keeps you polished!" Her eyes light up in recognition and she gives me that million-dollar smile, "Yes, of course. How wonderful to see you again." We reminisce about that brief time we spent in a hotel lobby in Phoenix, Arizona.

Only later do I realize how vividly that encounter has stayed with me. It's good to hold on to that kind of memory; it's a drop of sweetness that helps get you through life.

Up until now, ORLY's business has been geared toward the professional market selling to manicurists, salons and beauty supply stores. I'm not that interested in the consumer market, but in 1982 I decide to test the waters. I hire a sales representative who deals with the big retailers such as K-Mart and Walgreens to see what kind of response we might generate for a consumer version of our nail-strengthening product, the Romeo Kit.

The sales rep meets with the retail buyers. His pitch: "This is a professional product from ORLY that's unique. There's nothing like it in your stores. Why don't you try it out and see how it does?" And that was it; he comes back with big orders from K-Mart and Walgreens.

I think this looks like it's going to work out well…I have no idea how well. The answer is obvious when the first check arrives from

K-Mart. It's for $270,869.62. It's the largest check we've ever received for a single product. I feel like I'm sitting on top of the world.

...and then the unthinkable happens.

It's Friday night, September 17, 1982, the eve of the Jewish New Year, Rosh Hashanah. I leave work early. Even though we're not strictly observant, like most Jewish families we keep the traditions going by observing the High Holidays.

There's something profoundly satisfying about coming together with friends and family and performing the well-known rituals that unite us and make us feel how deeply connected we are to each other and to our faith. I pull into my driveway unaware of the tragic news that awaits me. The housekeeper opens the door and I know from the expression on her face that something terrible has happened.

How does a child—barely a toddler—find his way outside, through a gate and into the dangerous depths of a swimming pool? It's one of the many unanswerable questions that will haunt me the rest of my life. When I arrive at the hospital, Orly is in a state of shock. Dean, our nineteen-month-old son, our beautiful, smart, baby boy is in a coma from which he will never awaken. He will remain that way for five years before he finally lets go.

There are no words to describe what happens to a family that experiences such a tragedy. We torture ourselves with questions about "If-only's and should-have's." We suffer guilt, loss, anger, despair and a sadness so deep it feels like we will never come out of it. At best, Orly and I are surviving. We have two other sons to take care of and raise: Ran is seven and Tal is five. We need to think of them. I have a business to run and many employees. But my heart is not in any of it.

From that day on everything in my life changes. I have been so blessed, I've had so much success, a wonderful wife, a beautiful family and it gave me a feeling of self-worth, of great confidence. Now all of that is gone. I no longer trust life. I try to go back to work, but my mind is constantly distracted. I make errors in judgment. I'm unsure about my business dealings. Everything is a struggle.

The things that once gave meaning and direction to my life have become meaningless. Money, ambition, success; all have given way to a numbing sense of vulnerability.

I need to find a way to go on. Orly and I talk about going into therapy, but we can't bring ourselves to do it. We trust that our love will see us through. In retrospect, the devastation of our child's accident will prove to be far greater than we could imagine.

I find myself changed in many ways, some good, some not so good. I know for sure that money and success can't buy happiness. I regard people in a different light; they are no longer just names or faces. I see deeply into them as individuals and I know that everyone has experienced some kind of pain or suffering. I have a new understanding of the human condition.

I know that I am going through a major personal reassessment. With it comes an uncertainty that is having a negative effect on my business. I find myself depending on other people to take the reins and guide the future of ORLY.

Fortunately, I have many loyal employees who understand what my family and I are going through. Their sympathy and concern is comforting. It draws us closer together.

My wife, Orly, bears the worst of the burden; dealing every day with a child who is hovering between life and death. She holds on and prays that somewhere an answer will come, and that Dean will recover.

But no answer comes, only the growing acceptance of the inevitable.

People ask, "How did you get over it?" The answer is, "You don't. In time you learn to live with it. The rawness of the wound may heal but the scar remains forever."

Bit by bit, we pick up the pieces and try to be who we once were.

Outwardly it may seem like I am okay. In truth, I'm just trying to put one foot in front of the other. I search for any little spark of renewed interest that I can hang on to. I try to stay focused on work. Some days are better than others.

The company needs additional equipment and I find some used filling machines in Texas and have them shipped to our warehouse. The machines are in bad condition, but our trusted maintenance man, Glen Lazenby, can get them up and running. I'm grateful for something tangible to work on…something I know can fix. I get back to work.

The sales division is growing so rapidly that we decide to hire an assistant to take some of the load off our vice president of sales, Frank Caldwell. We start our search and interview several candidates, both male and female. It's been my hiring practice to find the best, most qualified person for the job, whether it's a man or a woman, and we are extremely fortunate to find Myriam Clifford. Myriam is bright, smart and has an extensive background in the beauty industry, most recently with Mary Kay products in Canada. I know she's destined to play an important part in the future of ORLY. Only time will reveal how important a role she will eventually play.

Even in my distracted state, the company continues to grow. Recognizing the tremendous value of consultants, I hire a third, Jim Brooks, who was previously a vice president of sales at Redken. Jim advises me on how to set up a sales department, how to package ORLY products, and how to approach new distributors.

I also start thinking about moving to a bigger warehouse space; 20,000 square feet is no longer adequate to accommodate our growing business. But I don't have the energy to do anything about it yet. Moving will have to wait.

In 1984, we find out that my wife, Orly, is pregnant again. We're sitting in the doctor's office waiting for the results of the sonogram when the doctor comes in with a big smile. "You're going to have a girl." Both our hearts leap with joy.

We are desperately in need of some happiness and a few months later, when our little girl, Shanee, arrives that's just what she brings—happiness and hope for the future. We begin to understand how insistent life is…how it goes on whether we want it to or not.

Photo of actress/model Brooke Shields given
personally to Jeff, February 1985.

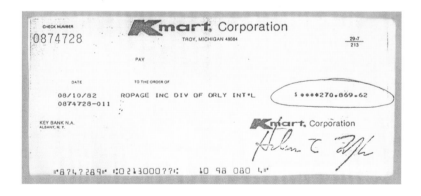

Orly's first big sale! Big check from K-Mart!
August 1982.

7

I PUT MYSELF TO THE TEST

With the birth of our daughter everything takes a turn for the better. Both Orly and I find a renewed interest in life. Once again, I resume the full responsibility for the day-to-day running of ORLY and things begin to return to some sense of order. That's when I get a phone call from a company called M.A.P. (Motivation and Performance) inviting me to attend a leadership seminar.

The man on the phone is warm and friendly and very convincing. I can tell right away that these people know their stuff. They've done their research and recognize ORLY as a company that is on the rise.

What they're offering is a three-day seminar to teach CEOs like me how to interact with our employees so that our companies will run more efficiently and our employees will find their jobs more satisfying.

Because ORLY was running smoothly, there was a great temptation not to rock the boat or make any changes. But to me that always seems like a sure way to get stuck in a rut. I never like to play it safe.

I have a tremendous curiosity about life, and I like to poke around in things to see what I can improve. I was intrigued by M.A.P.'s invitation and curious to learn what they could teach me.

I had about thirty employees at the time and I thought I had pretty great relationships with all of them. But I also knew I had benefited from working with consultants in the past, so I figured, "What the heck. Why not give it a try?"

I liked the M.A.P. approach as soon as they explained their methodology to me: "In two weeks, you'll come to our office in Newport Beach and attend a three-day seminar with about six or seven other CEOs. Before that, we'd like you to pick about a dozen of your key employees because we're going to send someone to your company to talk with them. We want to ask them questions about how they see the company and the way it's run. We guarantee them anonymity. That way, they're free to say whatever they think."

I sign up and a few days later, their interviewer shows up at ORLY headquarters. She is an intelligent, professional, and pleasant woman. I can see she will be easy to talk to. For the next few days, I give her a small office to work in where each of the twelve people I had recommended would meet with her.

As promised, I didn't know what she was asking or who was saying what. But I thought I knew my employees and I had a good feeling that they were saying positive things about me. I was really looking forward to hearing their comments.

Two weeks later, I drive to Newport Beach and sit down in a conference room with about seven other CEOs. They are all men, casually dressed, between the ages of thirty-five and fifty. They wear nice clothes, have expensive watches, stylish haircuts, and their nails are manicured (something that I definitely notice). Every one of them exudes the kind of confidence that comes from being the CEO of a successful company.

The seminar starts out in a very easy, relaxed manner. Introductions are made, and everyone is encouraged to say a few words about himself, his company, and what he hopes to gain from the seminar. It's obvious that we all take pride in our work and our ability to manage people and that most of us are here for the same reason: to learn new skills.

Then the seminar leader takes over. He's an energetic, extremely fit man in his late forties who looks as if he runs at least five miles a day. He starts out by praising us for the accomplishments that each of us has made in the business world. Then he explains that what we are about to learn might come as a surprise, but that we're not to let it trouble us in any way because at the end of the three days, we will see how this experience will change us all for the better.

His words cause a subtle but noticeable shift in the room. Things are getting a little uncomfortable.

On the mahogany conference table before us, he places a thick sheaf of papers. These papers, he explains, are the answers that our employees gave to their interviewers. He is going to call on each of us individually and read aloud what our employees said.

A slight feeling of apprehension fills the room. What if there are some negative comments? Did we want our dirty laundry aired in public? Well, it's too late to back out now.

The first CEO he focuses on is the head of a well-known toy company. He shows no emotion and doesn't move a muscle as the seminar leader launches into a recitation of what his employees said about him and his company.

It's painful to hear and each of us secretly prays that we will be spared such unflattering comments. No such luck. None of us come out unscathed.

When it's my turn, what I hear from my employees is that I don't appreciate what they do, I don't compliment them, I don't recognize their contributions, and they generally expect more from me.

It was devastating. In my mind, I thought we were getting along beautifully, but that's not what they said. Needless to say, every CEO in the room is shocked at what he hears. We all believe that we are the best bosses in the world. We can't imagine that our employees are so unhappy and that we are so unaware of it.

In truth, there were some positive comments about each of us...but what stuck in our minds were the criticisms of how we were failing in our leadership roles.

The seminar leader's assessment of my performance and that of all the other CEOs is that we were probably not managing our people very well. At the end of the first day, we were all licking our wounds—seven high-powered executives who had just gotten our butts kicked.

I go to bed that night with the words of my employees ringing in my ears...particularly hurtful is what they said about my "lack of appreciation." That was hard to take because the truth was that I felt enormous appreciation for them and what they did. All those negative comments kept replaying in my head. It didn't make for a very good night's sleep.

I knew from the syllabus they handed out that the following day they would start the training portion of the seminar on how to handle your employees. I'm looking forward to it because I can already see that what I'm learning in this seminar is going to be very impactful to me and to ORLY.

The next morning there is a completely different atmosphere in the conference room. None of us look confident. Instead, we all wear a similar look of determination. Each of us has thought long and hard about what we heard the day before and we've all had a similar reaction. It was tough to take, but we're all seasoned businessmen who know how to put our personal feelings aside and deal with the task at hand…which right now means learning how to be a better boss.

To our surprise, the seminar starts off not with an analysis of what our employees had said about us, but how we reacted to what was said. Every one of us completely ignored the fact that some positive observations were made about each of us and all we've focused on were the negative comments.

The leader nods knowingly, "And that's Lesson Number One. It's human nature. We all fear rejection; we all want praise." He then points out that we are no different than our employees or anyone else for that matter. We all crave acceptance and seek positive reinforcement for what we do; yet it's the negative feedback that always sticks in our minds.

We instantly recognize the truth in what he's saying because we each had experienced firsthand how the criticisms we received from our employees had consumed us, while whatever praise they gave us had been completely ignored.

"So," he goes on, "what you need to know is how to make it comfortable for people to accept criticism." He then lays out a familiar scenario that we've all encountered.

"Let's assume you call someone into your office. You start the conversation by saying, 'Joe, you made a big mistake.' Right away, you've lost him. The minute you start with something negative he's no longer with you. Nobody wants to hear bad things.

"So what's the right way to do it? When Joe comes into your office, you start by praising his work. 'Joe, you've been working for me for three or four years now. You've done a wonderful job and I definitely want you to know that I appreciate what you do and that you're a very good employee.' The minute you say this to him, he's open to hearing anything, even criticism. Then you say, 'But you know, the other day when you did such and such…I don't think it was the right way to handle it and if I was in your place, I would have done it differently.' Now he's listening to you. But if you start from the beginning of the conversation by criticizing him, without preparing him, you've lost him. He's on the defensive and he's not going hear what you have to say. Instead, he's busy thinking how he's going to justify his actions. He might even argue and that's not going to fix the problem."

I know right away that this is one of the most important lessons I am going to take away from the seminar and I know it's going to change the way I communicate with my employees.

The second lesson he teaches us is that the way to handle our employees is to truly appreciate the job they do for you and to let them know it at every opportunity. He drives the lesson home by saying, "If you can compliment someone ten times a day then do it, because if you tell a person something good only one time, they'll forget it. But if you tell them something bad only one time, they'll remember it forever."

What he emphasizes is that in order to run a company where our employees are going to be loyal and appreciative, you can never stop praising them. This seems almost simplistic and obvious, but in hearing it, it opens our eyes to a way of dealing with our employees that most of us were not even aware of, or thought we were doing already. From the feedback I received from the interviews, that was clearly not the case.

For the final day of the seminar, we're asked to write up a statement on how we plan to implement what we've learned over the three days. I draw up a plan and can't wait to put it into action.

On the day I come back into the office, I call my twelve key employees, who were interviewed by M.A.P., into the boardroom. When they arrive, I can see they're a little hesitant. Maybe they're thinking that I'm bringing them together to complain about what they said to the interviewer. Maybe they're concerned that their jobs are in jeopardy. They all seem nervous.

Then I break the ice and say, "I want to thank everyone who was interviewed for being honest and open by saying exactly how you feel about the way I do things around here. I have no idea who said what because your answers were kept completely anonymous. The seminar was wonderful, very eye opening. I learned some valuable lessons that are going to change the way ORLY is run and the first thing I want to do is let you know how much I appreciate each one of you and all the great things you do for this company. I may not always say it, but I am always aware of how much you care about ORLY and how loyal and hard-working you all are. I want you to keep bringing me your ideas, keep bringing me your creative input. This is the beginning of a whole new way of working together and I can't imagine a better group of people to be working with."

Right away I can see that my sincere words of praise have lightened the mood. There are a lot of smiles and very positive feelings in the room. From that day on everything changed—for myself and for the company. It took no effort. All I had to do was keep the lines of communication open and to express whatever gratitude I honestly felt and immediately I could see people blossoming with pride.

Three months after I attended the seminar, the M.A.P. interviewer came back to interview the same twelve people again. This time she shares with me the question she is going to ask, "Do you see any difference between the way Jeff treats you now and the way he did in the past?" The response is unanimous. Everyone says the difference is like night and day.

M.A.P. gives me the results of their second round of interviews and when I read what wonderful things my employees said about the way I was treating them, it was very gratifying

There's no doubt in my mind that the leadership seminar was the best thing I could have done because it changed the way I ran ORLY. It created a more open and constructive relationship between my employees and me as well as among the employees themselves because they felt we were becoming one cohesive company. That was over thirty years ago, and that culture of praise is still true of ORLY today.

Because of the relationships that I've established with my employees, I can honestly say that between what I learned in the M.A.P. seminar and my own hiring instincts, I have rarely ever had to fire anyone for not doing their job.

I know that if someone is having a hard time in their personal life it may be reflected in their work. That's when it becomes even more important to be understanding and supportive and to encourage people to talk about what's going on with them and more importantly, to learn how to listen. I may not have the answers to all their problems but at least they know they have my ear and my sympathy.

I promise you, it's far more effective than any reprimand or warning.

At the end of 1985 and after five years of working for me, Frank Caldwell, the vice president of sales, decides he wants to freelance as a consultant. Frank has been a valuable employee but waiting to fill his shoes is the very capable Myriam Clifford. Myriam has been Frank's assistant for two years and I've been keeping my eye on her. I know she will do a great job as the new director of sales. ORLY is already moving up into a top position in the nail industry and I know I can trust Myriam to keep us on track.

8

GO WITH YOUR GUT

It's 1986 and we're already outgrowing our 20,000 square feet of warehouse space. That's when I find a building in Chatsworth on Deering Avenue not far from our present location. The building is twice as big, and it will be perfect for our expanding company. As ORLY continues to grow, it means more individuals to deal with and more challenges to face.

Our operations director, Nancy Smet, is very efficient at her job and always wants things to be exactly right. One morning, Nancy comes into my office and I can see right away how upset she is. Her hands are shaking and I'm afraid that she's going to spill her coffee all over my desk. "Nancy, sit down. What's wrong?"

"Jeff we're going to have to fire Glen."

This is not good news. Glen Lazenby is our head of maintenance. He takes care of everything related to the warehouse and the machinery. He's been with ORLY a long time. He's excellent at his job and can fix anything, plus he's always coming up with creative solutions. That's exactly the kind of employee I like. In my eyes, Glen is indispensable. "Why? What's going on?" I ask Nancy.

Nancy is a very capable young woman but sometimes she can be a little rigid. She knows the rules and sticks to them and if one of the employees doesn't follow the rules, she takes it very personally.

"I don't know what else to do, Jeff. I've told Glen time and time again about coming in late. He has to be here before everyone else in order to get the plant up and running. If he's not here by six-thirty, it puts everyone behind schedule. And now he's coming in late almost every morning. Today he was an hour late. It's creating a real problem."

She's right. That is a problem. But I'm definitely not eager to get rid of Glen. He'd be hard to replace.

"Did you ask him why he's late all the time?"

"Yes. But he keeps coming up with the same bullshit excuse. His car won't start."

Nancy is at the end of her rope. I can see she's angry and the last thing I want is for two of my employees to be against each other. It's the kind of problem that spills over into gossip and rumors. Then other people get involved. I don't want any of that. I know I have to step in before it gets out of hand. "Let me talk to Glen. Tell him to come to my office tomorrow morning."

Nancy leaves with a sense of relief at having handed her problem over to me. She may be right about his car excuse, but I know from my own experience what it's like to deal with a bad car, so I'm able to be a little more sympathetic.

I think back to an old Buick that I bought for $250 from Jack Sperling's mother. Every time it rained the car filled up with water. Jack and I always joked that the best way to deal with it was to wear a bathing suit on rainy days. So I'm willing to consider that Glen's car troubles might be real.

That night I give the problem a lot of thought, and by the next morning, I've come up with a solution. At 8:00 a.m., Glen comes into my office. He's a big, imposing guy with a lot of self-confidence. I know he loves his job, but he won't let anybody mess with him.

He's the kind of man who, if he feels wrongly accused or mistreated, would just as soon walk away. He's a lot like me in that way. I don't beat around the bush. I come straight to the point. "Glen, what's this problem you're having with your car?"

"It's an old car, Jeff. Sometimes it's the battery; sometimes it's the ignition. You know me, Jeff, I can fix anything, but every morning…that car…I'm not sure if it's even going to start, and some days it's harder to get it going than others. Yesterday it took me almost an hour. That's why I was late for work."

He tells me this story in an open and honest way that makes me believe he's telling the truth. I know for sure he's the kind of guy who'll squeeze every drop of life out of that car before he'll give up on it. I admire that. It's that kind of determination that makes him such a valuable employee. I think for a minute before I propose my idea.

"Glen, what if ORLY could help you buy a better car?" He jerks his head back in surprise and narrows his eyes.

"Really?"

"Sure, get something reasonably priced that the company could pay for and then you can pay it back a little at a time." An uncertain smile lights his face and he shakes his head in disbelief.

"Wow, Jeff, I don't know what to say."

I assure him it's strictly a business arrangement and that it will be good for both of us. I can see the look of amazement on Glen's face and I know that he came into my office thinking I might fire him. He's not quite sure how to deal with this unexpected turn of events. I reach out to shake his hand and he clasps my hand in both of his. "I don't know exactly how, Jeff, but I promise I'll pay you back."

"Don't worry about it. I'll talk to the CFO and we'll work something out for you."

He leaves stammering. "Thank you, Jeff…thank you so much."

A few minutes later, Nancy shows up to see how things went. When she hears the deal I made with Glen, her jaw drops. She looks at me with disdain, "Well, that was a waste of money!"

I nod solemnly, "You might be right, Nancy, but let's give it a couple weeks and see what happens." She gives me a "Hmph!" and leaves.

Two weeks go by…then three…then four. I don't hear another word about Glen's tardiness. Then at the end of the month Nancy pokes her head in my door wearing a sheepish grin. "Jeff, I want to apologize. You were right about Glen. He hasn't been late a single day since he got the new car. I must say it's changed my opinion of him. He's a lot more reliable than I gave him credit for. My hat's off to you, Jeff. I would have fired him."

I resist the urge to say, "I told you so," and recognize that this is a far more important moment for Nancy, where she can learn a valuable lesson. I invite her to come in and sit down. "I'll tell you the truth, Nancy, I wasn't really sure my plan would work. It easily could have gone the other way…but sometimes you gotta go with your gut and take a chance on people."

Nancy gets it. She smiles and nods, "I'll remember that, Jeff."

In the end, I was glad my belief in Glen had paid off, not only for the company but for Nancy, too. Within a few months she and Glen (the very same guy that she wanted to fire) started dating, and within two years they were married.

I love a story with such a happy ending.

9

HOLY COW!

By the 1990s, ORLY has 40,000 square feet of warehouse space and almost fifty employees. We now enjoy the status of being number one in the professional nail care industry. Not only do we have a successful nail polish line, but our unique nail care treatments dominate the market and become the trademark of ORLY.

My love of tinkering in the laboratory has proven to be a great asset. After creating Romeo, Ridgefiller, and The French Manicure, I developed an entire line of nail strengtheners and treatment products that address different types of nail problems. Among them are Nail Defense, Calcium Shield, Nail Armor, Bonder Base Coat, Cuticle Remover, Quick Dry Top Coat, Cuticle Therapy Crème, Clean Prep, Cuticle Oil, and Argan Cuticle and Hand Cream.

One of these products came about in an interesting way. My father had eczema. Whenever I went to visit him in Israel, I would bring him a product called Cuticura which was known for treating eczema. One day he said, kind of as a joke, "You're as smart as any chemist. Why do you have to buy products from other companies? Why don't you make me something for my skin?" I always like a challenge, so I said, "I'll do it!"

When I got home, I went to a well-known laboratory in Hollywood and asked them to develop a very rich product that would remedy my father's eczema. And they did it. They came up with an amazing product, which I made just for him. I didn't make it for the market. But then I found that it worked on dry cuticles. I decided to make the same thing for the manicurists and call it Cuticle Therapy Cream. It became a big seller, and it remedied my father's eczema, too.

I was gaining a reputation as a guy who knew how to come up with creative ideas and solutions to nail care problems. That's why I've always enjoyed the marketing side of the business; it's one of the places where you can really let your imagination run wild, which is just what I did with our next big product.

Once or twice a year, all the beauty product manufacturers get together at major trade shows and roll out our new products. The biggest show is held during the summer in Las Vegas. Every manufacturer sets up exhibits there and it's always a challenge to stand out from the crowd. Hundreds of new products are introduced every year accompanied by a lot of hoopla designed to grab the attention of potential customers who, after the first day, are generally wandering around on the trade show floor glassy-eyed from overload.

In 1993, I introduced my newest creation: the Calcium Shield. This was an alternate version of our very successful Nail Defense, a protein-based strengthener that fortified brittle nails. One of the things we understand at ORLY is that just like with shampoos and face creams, not every product works the same on every one of us. You have to keep putting out new products for the individual customer to try and see what is best for them.

As calcium is the foundation of hair and nails, I had been developing an idea revolving around some women having better results with a calcium-based strengthener than with our protein-based Nail Defense. I came up with a product called the Calcium Shield. There's only so much explaining and handing out samples that you can do at a trade show without becoming just another one of the many exhibitors who are filling up people's goodie bags and vying for attention.

For a few weeks before the convention, I kept thinking about how I could get people to take notice of the Calcium Shield. I needed something eye-catching, something that would get people talking. I was drawing lots of blanks. Then one night I was sitting at the dinner table and Orly was pouring one of the kids a glass of milk and it struck me, "Where does a major source of calcium come from? Milk." In a flash, I realized that what I needed for the trade show in Las Vegas was a cow.

"Jeff, are you crazy?" That's how Orly responded. That's how my marketing people responded. "Yes, I am crazy…and I need a cow." The next day my marketing team crowded into my office. "How are you going to get a cow onto the convention floor?" "Who's going to give you permission to do that?" "There's got to be health laws against it."

I raised my hand to stop them. "Who knows? We'll figure it out. You just get me the cow."

I was confident that the marketing department would come up with a cow in time for the show but convincing the show producer to let me bring a cow into the convention hall, that was up to me.

In the 1990s, hair products were really the mainstay of all beauty product shows. But I know that any decent promoter is always looking for ways to expand his business and attract other product manufacturers—not just hair care manufacturers—so that was how I pitched the cow to the show producer. I assured him that this clever promotion, featuring a live cow, was sure to draw a lot of welcome attention to his show, plus it would open the way for nail products to become an important feature of his future shows rather than an afterthought to hair care products.

It was a lot easier to convince him than I had imagined. He went for it right away and made all the necessary arrangements for me to bring a cow into the Las Vegas Convention Center.

With everything set to go, all I need is the cow.

A few days later, my marketing people put me in touch with a cattle rancher in the Las Vegas area. I call him up and he explains to me that the convention center isn't really set up for large animals. He suggests that it might be better for me to have a calf. I like that idea; calves are cute…people love them.

We still need a fence around our exhibition space, bales of hay, a straw floor and an attendant to stand by for clean up, but that all sounds perfectly doable to me. "Can people pet the calf?" I ask. "Sure thing, they can even feed her from a bottle."

That's it! I can see it already—everyone wanting to bottle-feed a baby calf! It's a done deal.

The opening day of the convention, my calf arrives. She's a beautiful little black and white spotted Holstein, with soulful eyes and lashes that would be the envy of any woman. Needless to say, she's the hit of the show.

The whole convention is talking about ORLY. Visiting our booth and feeding the calf becomes "a must" for everyone on the floor. We put a little lightweight saddle on her back with the words "The Calcium Shield" and our new product is a sensation.

True to my prediction, the calf makes it into all the news stories about the trade show, and that "crazy guy" Jeff Pink is the talk of the town. From that day on, nail products become a much more prominent feature in all beauty product trade shows.

That wasn't the end of my convention antics. You remember my great friend Jack Sperling, the man who got me started in the beauty products business? Another year, he and I were at a convention where Jack was offering a promotion: if you bought $20,000 in product from him you would get a free Vespa, a very popular European motor scooter.

Jack's Vespa was bright yellow and prominently displayed in his booth; it was a thing of beauty. I had driven motor scooters all over Israel, so I told Jack, "Jump on the back and I'll take you for a ride around the convention floor." Jack looked at me like I'd lost my mind. "You're crazy, Jeff. We can't do that!"

"Yes. I am crazy, so let's do it."

We jump on the Vespa and take off, waving to all our friends as we whizz by. People can't believe what they're seeing. I'm racing up and down the aisles, managing not to hit anyone and having a great time when suddenly we pass two security guards standing at their post beside the entrance doors.

Their heads whip around in disbelief as we fly by, and it takes them a few seconds before they realize what they've just seen. They take off after us on foot shouting, "Stop! Stop!" but they're no match for the Vespa. I yell to Jack, "Hold on tight and get ready to jump off." We zoom down the aisles into his booth and leap off the bike. Jack has a big sheet that he throws over the Vespa and we quickly cover it and stand at the booth as if we're just casually talking. The two guards arrive huffing and puffing and ask us if we've seen two guys on a motorbike. In unison Jack and I point toward the exit, "They went that way." Once again, we're the talk of the show.

Our reputation for being the bad boys of the conventions precedes us and for the next show in New Orleans, just for fun, we rent a limousine, fill it with a band of street musicians, and drive through the town with a trumpet, a clarinet, and a trombone all poking out the windows and playing some hot New Orleans jazz while Jack and I shake our tambourines.

By now Jack Sperling and I have become closer than ever. We enjoy each other's company and we share a lot of history. We both know that no matter where our lives take us, we can always count on each other; we'll always have each other's backs.

Jeff feeds the little calf in the ORLY exhibitor booth
at the Las Vegas Beauty Show (BBSI), 1993.

Jeff riding a Vespa in the exhibition booth aisles of the
Las Vegas Beauty Show (BBSI), 1993.

Two perfect displays of Jack Sperling's unique sense of humor
while picking Jeff up at the airport with Cindy Cebulak.

10

THE BIG MOVE

"Myriam, I want to make you president of ORLY."

I t's 1994 and I've made a major decision. I'm moving the family to Israel and I want Myriam Clifford to run the company for me. Myriam has been with ORLY for eleven years, has been the vice president of sales since 1990, and has done an outstanding job.

She's sitting in my office contemplating my offer with her fingers pressed together. She takes her time answering. I'm impatient to know. "Well, are you interested?" A questioning smile spreads across her face. "Exactly what do you have in mind, Jeff?"

I explain to her that ever since I started developing the international market for ORLY, I've been thinking that it would be good if I spent more time somewhere that was closer to our overseas customers.

I outline how things could work; she will be the president of ORLY in charge of the day-to-day operations. I'll remain the CEO and stay in charge of International Sales and I'll be available to consult with her on anything of importance, plus I'll return frequently to make sure I know everything that is going on.

She accepts and within a few weeks we finalize the deal and the matter is settled.

This is not something I've done on a whim. I'd been thinking seriously about it for a couple of years. It's about more than just business. My wife Orly and I have talked a lot about going back to Israel. She has a real fear of earthquakes and after the big Northridge earthquake in January 1994, she had a terrifying dream about seeing herself buried alive. She definitely wants to leave California.

Our older son Ran is already in college. He'll stay in the U.S. and continue his studies while our second son, Tal, finishes his last year of high school at the American School in Israel. Our daughter Shanee is ten and will continue her studies in Israel. It will be a good opportunity for her to learn Hebrew. We come up with a lot of compelling reasons to make this move and we do it.

Even though we've been in the U.S. long enough to feel like its home, moving back to Israel is returning to our roots. It's easy for us to make the adjustment because we both have family and friends around us. We find a nice house in the suburbs of Tel Aviv and settle in.

Businesswise, things are going very well. I'm able to move easily between Israel and Europe and the ORLY products are flourishing in the international market.

Unfortunately, our marriage is in trouble. The tragedy of losing our son, Dean, is ten years behind us and even though Orly and I have worked very hard to go on with our lives, we both feel that something fundamental has been lost.

I've always believed that for a marriage to last, it has to have three things: love, respect, and trust. There's no doubt that we have respect and trust for each other, but we both recognize that somewhere along the way the love we once had has been lost.

Orly and I decide to divorce. It's a difficult decision and we don't do it with anger and emotion. We talk about it endlessly. It's hard for both of us to accept that after twenty years, our marriage is coming to an end.

We want to do it in a way that will not cause suffering to the children. Neither of us is in any rush to find another partner. We agree to take our time, and we do our best to make our divorce as amicable as possible, but we both know it's for the best. Once the divorce is finalized, we will be going our separate ways.

It's an uneasy time, and to be honest, I know that I haven't been paying as much attention as I should have to the ORLY operations in the United States. With the international market for ORLY products well established, there is nothing to keep me in Israel and I decide it's time to move back to Los Angeles.

I'm looking forward to getting back to my old routine. I have no idea what's waiting for me.

It's a true fall day; crisp, clear and a little chilly; the kind of day we don't get too often in Los Angeles. Even though I have been back to ORLY many times since the move to Israel, this morning, as I drive the familiar streets to our headquarters in Chatsworth, I have mixed feelings. Coming back to oversee the day-to-day operations of a company that I left in the hands of Myriam Clifford and other senior management for four years will take some adjusting on everyone's part.

How will my executives react? Will it be like having your parents move in with you when you're already an adult? I don't want to diminish their positions or commitment to the company. I anticipate that it's going to be a tricky situation and that I'll need to pay close attention to it.

I pull into the parking lot and slip into my assigned space. Suddenly, I feel a stirring of that old excitement about coming to work and all my concerns disappear. It's as if I can feel my creative juices starting to flow again and I'm eager to get back to developing new products for ORLY.

I bound up the stairs with a burst of energy. Fortunately, with all the tennis and regular yoga classes, I've kept in good physical shape for a man of fifty-four and I'm barely breathing hard as I stride across the jam-packed warehouse floor. I note that after nine years in this 40,000-square-foot building, ORLY is practically bursting at the seams. I smile at the thought that we might be ready to make another big change.

I'm walking at a brisk pace as I enter the conference room where Myriam and about twelve other senior staff have gathered for my arrival. After an initial round of hand shaking and welcome-back greetings, they all return to their work except for Myriam and her three top executives.

Right away I notice no one is looking me in the eyes. Myriam is seated at the conference table, scribbling in a notebook. The others are stirring their coffee or checking their cell phones. I sense that something strange is happening...but what?

I look around trying to assess the situation...no clues. Finally, I just ask directly, "Okay, Myriam, so tell me what's going on here?"

She stops writing and laces her fingers together on top of a blue report folder. She takes a deep breath and finally looks up at me. I can see fear in her eyes. "Jeff, I'll be honest with you. We didn't want to worry you about this, but we're having a problem with a couple of our big retailers."

Myriam is not someone who exaggerates, and I know that she believes that most problems are just challenges to be overcome, so her concern has a big impact on me. Everyone else in the room is very quiet. "How big a problem?" I ask.

She pushes the blue report toward me. "It's big, Jeff. Really big."

I open the report and glance over the colorful pie charts and graphs that translate the financial condition of ORLY into an easy-to-read picture. It only takes a cursory glance for me to see that all the signs are pointing in the wrong direction. I close the folder. I don't need to see anymore. What I do need is to hear what the hell happened.

Myriam starts, "We're taking a big hit on the returns from our retail customers." As Myriam goes on to explain the difficult situation that ORLY is in, her voice recedes in the distance and I am thrust back into the discussions we've had over the past year.

Myriam was very eager to expand ORLY into the consumer market. A big change was occurring in the nail polish world in the early 1990s. In the past, nail polish colors were predominantly dark with the biggest sellers being red, maroon, or brown. But in the '90s new pastel colors like pinks, beiges, creams, and blues were introduced and were in great demand by consumers. The entire market was opening up in new ways and we were in danger of being left out. Our competitors had all jumped on the bandwagon and as a result ORLY was slipping out of our long-cherished number one position.

Moving aggressively into the retail market was a difficult decision for me. Even though we'd done some lucrative deals back in the 1980s with Walgreens and K-Mart, I've always been hesitant about the consumer market. It ran counter to my desire to make ORLY into a first-class professional product sold mainly to nail salons and beauty supply stores. But it was important to Myriam and the idea of expanding into the consumer market with a line of trendy fashion colors was her baby. She brought in a sales representative to speak with me who knew that market well and was convinced that he could generate healthy orders for ORLY. Myriam was reading the writing on the wall and she wanted to get in on the booming market.

After giving it serious consideration, I agreed to let her try it, mainly because I didn't want to kill her initiative. I've always believed that it's important for the employees who are running your company to be personally invested with their own ideas. It brings a certain passion to their work and that's what I've always wanted ORLY to reflect—how much everyone in the company cares about what the name ORLY stands for.

So I gave Myriam a green light to go to the retail market with a new line of fashion colors, and in a few short months, she proved herself right. At first it was very successful. The sales rep delivered huge orders from several big drug store chains and Myriam hired him to be vice president of sales.

The results were extremely profitable, and everything seemed to be on track. But after a year or two, fashions changed and the pastel colors were no longer in demand; now it was dark greens and blues, and next season it would be gold and silver. Two of our biggest retail customers wanted to return the pastel colors because they weren't selling anymore. That's where the problem started.

Now Myriam is telling me a horror story that is just beginning to sink in. "We've never had anyone do this before, Jeff, and we just didn't see it coming."

The truth is, no one in the company did. We all were aware of how "shelf space management" worked, how companies like ORLY had to pay for shelf space in order to guarantee their products would be seen. We also knew that if a product was underperforming, a new company could bid for your shelf space. When that happened, the common practice was that the new company would buy off the old products and dispose of them however they wished, or the retailer would absorb them and sell them off to liquidators.

But these mega-drugstores, instead of absorbing unsold merchandise the way that Walgreens and K-Mart did, had inserted a "return and refund" clause into their contracts, which had gone unnoticed. We hadn't read the fine print and didn't realize the possible consequences of this clause.

What it meant was that we were obligated to pay back all the money we had been paid in advance for unsold inventory, and that whatever was left on the shelves was shipped back to us. Worst of all, it was returned in an extremely insulting manner.

Hundreds of thousands of nail polish bottles had been unceremoniously dumped into shipping containers. Many of the bottles had broken so that their contents spilled out and destroyed the rest of the products, rendering the entire shipment unusable. Not only were we taking a hit on the cash refunds, we were losing millions of dollars in the return of damaged goods. My first instinct was to challenge the legality of the contract, but our lawyers declared the "return and refund" clause binding.

Myriam was right; we'd never had anything like this happen. In the past the only products we sold to the consumer market were The French Manicure and the Romeo Kit. Those both had long shelf lives and unlike seasonal nail polishes, we never had any returns. We had made a serious error because we were operating in uncharted waters. What we needed to do immediately was to stop the bleeding.

I set up meetings with the buyers at the two mega-pharmacies who were the major offenders. I walked in to find that the buyers were young, fresh-faced women I had never seen before. They probably had less than five years' experience between them.

Both meetings went the same way. I told them that ORLY would not be doing any further business with them and that we would not take any more returns. They would need to sell off our shelf space to another company who would assume any leftover ORLY products.

The first buyer I met with was dumbfounded; she couldn't understand why I was so upset. "We love your products, Jeff; the quality is excellent and they do very well here."

"So, if you love my products so much, why did you return them like they were nothing but a pile of useless trash?" She had no answer for that.

The other buyer tried to take a more business-like approach. "Jeff, you know that nail polish is a seasonal item. We just can't afford to keep that much old product on hand. We need to have constant turnover of new product."

Despite her logical argument, I could hear a note of regret in her voice. She knew that she couldn't defend her company's policy but that was her job. "That's nice," I replied. "You make money on my products and I lose money. What kind of a deal is that?"

I could see that both these buyers had no loyalty to me or to ORLY. They were only interested in making money for their bosses, and they were afraid of losing their jobs if they didn't. And they were right to be afraid.

The job turnover in the big drugstore chains can make your head spin. It's hard to find a buyer or merchandiser who's been there more than two or three years. As a supplier, we're constantly having to educate new buyers on how highly regarded the name ORLY is, and that we're at the forefront of product innovation, that every product—from our nail treatments to our polishes—is held to rigorously high standards which have become our hallmark in the industry.

What really irritated me was the complete disrespect for the products that we had put our lifeblood into and which they had shipped back like garbage.

No one from either company ever bothered to apologize. It was the end of our relationship with both giant companies and a hard lesson learned about reading the fine print…a lesson that came with a price tag of several million dollars.

11

THE WAY THE COOKIE CRUMBLES

The financial losses ORLY suffered in 1998 aren't large enough to put us entirely out of business, but we can't pay our vendors or maintain the high salaries of our top executives. I accept Myriam Clifford's resignation and vow to never again let the company get so far away from my personal attention

As soon as our executive team learns that ORLY is in big trouble, they start putting out feelers for other jobs. Big companies eagerly snatch up most of the top people and Myriam ends up working as a consultant for my former distributor, Spilo. It's a very small world.

The management team is reduced from twenty to eight and suddenly I'm back to where I was twenty years ago. Now it's just me with a small team, and we're struggling to keep the doors open.

I try to keep a cool head and make an honest assessment of where we stand, but there's no avoiding the truth: ORLY is in crisis. I need to take action, and as I've always done in difficult times, I look for advice from my closest associates. The first stop is a visit to my CPA firm.

It's an unusually gray day and it reflects my mood. At 10:00 a.m. I'm seated in a wood-paneled conference room facing three somber-looking accountants in dark suits. They're well aware of what's going on since they've been with me for fifteen years—almost from the time I started ORLY. It's their job to prepare my annual reports and they've seen the numbers and know what a disastrous nosedive ORLY is in.

The head of the CPA firm is a patronizing, fatherly figure. I've put up with him through the years because his firm does good work for us. Now he's looking at me with an attitude of defeat and resignation. "Jeff, our advice is that you file for Chapter Eleven." His words are like a knife through my heart.

"BANKRUPTCY?! You're advising me to declare ORLY bankrupt?"

The three heads nod in agreement. "It's the only way, Jeff. It will make all your debts go away and you'll be able to start fresh." Again they nod in unison while the head of the firm shrugs apologetically. I've heard enough. I jump to my feet. "Don't ever say anything like that about ORLY!"

Who the hell is this pissant number cruncher to equate ORLY with failure? The very idea that I would declare bankruptcy is so infuriating that I can't even discuss it. I'm done with this idiot. I lean toward his pasty, sallow face. "If that's the best advice you have for me, you're fired!"

The three heads stammer and look at each other in nervous confusion. I don't wait for their response. I grab my briefcase and leave, incensed at their stupidity and enraged by their insensitivity...as if ORLY was nothing more than a collection of failing numbers on a page of their lifeless ledgers.

I return home overwhelmed with a kind of loneliness that I have never experienced before. In the past, no matter what sort of difficulties I encountered, I knew I had Orly to talk to. She may not always have had answers for me, but she always listened with a sympathetic ear and it helped me sort things out.

I realize how much I miss that. I need to talk to someone. I need some better advice than what my accountants dished out. I call my friend and lawyer, Steve Wasserman.

Steve and I have known one another for a long time. We met in a courtroom in 1985 where Steve was the defense attorney in a lawsuit that I had brought against one of his clients. Steve did a very good job defending his client, but the judge ruled in my favor. After the case was settled, Steve and I started talking and we liked each other, so we began working together.

I eventually learned that Steve's easy-going personality was responsible for attracting many clients to his law firm, including me. He had that rare quality that's a necessity in every business; he knew how to schmooze and bring clients into his firm.

Today, Steve doesn't litigate cases; he leaves that up to his two partners and a roster of high-priced lawyers. But he's always there for me when I need him—as a friend, legal advisor, and in many ways, business consultant.

I can't count how many times we've gone to lunch together. Sometimes it's about business but more often it's just to catch up on what has become a long-lasting friendship.

All it takes is one phone call and Steve and I are seated across from each other at our favorite Chinese restaurant. He pours the tea and I pour out my story about the desperate situation that ORLY is in. Steve listens quietly. He doesn't feel compelled to react to anything. He's taking it all in and I know his response will be measured and above all, helpful. Just talking to him makes me feel better.

I talk all through the wonton soup and by the time we've finished the broccoli and beef, I've laid out all the grim details of how ORLY got into such deep trouble, including the bad advice I got from my accountants to declare bankruptcy.

Finally, Steve looks at me in that straight-forward way he has and says "Jeff, listen, you're not going to go into Chapter Eleven. I know you; you're too smart, and you're too resourceful. Besides, ninety percent of the companies that go into Chapter Eleven never come back. You're gonna find another way to deal with this."

It was like he lifted an elephant off my chest. I took the first deep breath I'd taken in days. Steve did what good friends do; he said the right thing at the right time and ended all my doubts about what I would do next.

Over another pot of tea and some fortune cookies, I tell Steve an idea I've been thinking about.

"What if I contact all my vendors, the ones I've worked with for so many years, and ask them to help me out? Maybe I can make some kind of a long-term arrangement with them to give me enough time so that I can pay them back."

Steve likes the idea. "Sure, why not? What's the worst they can do? Say no? I'll bet you most of them will go along with it. They know your reputation and they know if you make a promise, you'll be good for it." He hands me my fortune cookie. "Here, you haven't opened it."

I crack it apart, take out the little slip of paper and read it aloud. "You are admired by everyone for your talent and ability."

"See," says Steve, "fortune cookies don't lie."

The next day, I sit down and draft a letter to my vendors, twenty-five in all, explaining the financial situation we're in. It's not easy. I have to swallow my pride and admit to the mistakes I've made. But after so many years, I've learned how to roll with the punches and I know that the best thing to do is to put my personal feelings aside and deal with the situation in a very straightforward and business-like way. I dive in and write the letter.

Dear _____:

Because you have been our trusted partner for many years, I'm writing to let you know that ORLY is dealing with a financial emergency that will temporarily impact our ability to pay our creditors. Due to an unexpected product return we now find ourselves facing a cash flow crisis that could result in the permanent closing of ORLY and the defaulting of all our outstanding debts. If that were to happen, the most our creditors might realize would be 10 cents on the dollar.

WE ARE DETERMINED NOT TO LET THIS HAPPEN!

We are grateful for the many years we have worked with you and your company and are proud of the high regard that ORLY enjoys as a trusted leader and innovator in the nail products industry. We do not intend to violate that trust by passing on our losses to you. Instead we will do everything in our power to assure the continuing future of ORLY and to guarantee that as our assets recover, you will receive every dollar that is coming to you.

In light of that, I would like to propose a possible solution that will require some patience and understanding on your part, but in the end will provide a positive outcome to all parties involved. We anticipate that within a three-year time period we will once again be solvent enough to pay off all our creditors. If you will set aside our current debt and continue to work with us, we promise to pay you in full as soon as we are back on our feet.

We are eager to discuss the terms of this agreement with you at your earliest convenience and thank you for your consideration.

I look forward to your reply.

Jeff Pink

CEO, ORLY

It takes less than an hour to write the letter but when I'm finished, I feel that I've struck the right balance—that it's both humble and confident, and that I've taken the first step in my own recovery. I look outside my office at the warehouse floor where the noisy interaction of packaging and shipping, conveyor belts, and forklifts go on as if nothing has happened. And that's how I want it to be. I don't want the general workforce to know how close we are to the edge of financial disaster.

Those who need to know have already been told. As far as the rest of the company is concerned, ORLY is doing just fine. They don't need to know that in a few short days we'll start running out of the supplies needed to replenish our stock of bottles, brushes, caps, boxes, and all the miscellaneous packaging items needed to build up our inventory.

Unless the vendors agree to keep supplying us, everything will come to a grinding halt. I don't want to even think about having to tell these loyal, hard-working people that it's over.

Only a few middle-management people remain, and I decide to sit down with each of them and explain the positive steps I'm taking to secure their future with ORLY.

I assure them that I will use every means possible to make sure that ORLY stays in business, and that I'm positive we will weather this storm. The bad news is that it requires everyone to take a temporary pay cut. I let them know that if they feel they have to look elsewhere for work, I understand.

I can see in each of their faces the difficult choice they are facing. They have families to feed, bills to pay. I give them each a few days to think about it and to let me know their decision.

The one person who doesn't need any time to think about it is Veronica Reyes. At that time, Veronica was the Controller and would eventually become the CFO. She had started at ORLY as

Myriam Clifford's right-hand woman. Veronica is a petite Filipina, a dynamo with a natural affinity for numbers and a comprehensive overview of how the company runs. She proves her fierce loyalty to ORLY by insisting that she will do anything it takes to help turn things around.

"I believe in you, Jeff," she says. "You've never let anyone down and I know you'll bring ORLY back bigger than ever." Like Steve Wasserman, Veronica has said the right thing at the right time. Never have I been more grateful for the support and encouragement of any employee, and I'm all too aware that this petite, 5'2" woman is committed to holding me up with all her strength. Immediately, I turn over a lot more responsibility to her and she eagerly rises to the challenge. Veronica and I will be overseeing every aspect of ORLY until we can afford to hire additional managers.

Within a few days, I hear back from all the vendors I sent letters to. The news is good. My carefully chosen words have hit the mark. All but one of my vendors indicates they're willing to consider my request. I'll have to speak individually with the head of each company to finalize the agreements but already I can see a faint glimmer of light at the end of the tunnel. I begin to believe that this is all going to work out.

The next morning, I dress for my first meeting, choosing my wardrobe carefully. There's a lot at stake here and my personal appearance needs to make the right impression: confident, serious, but nothing that reads as excessive. I pick a pair of well-creased tan pants, a white shirt, and a tweed Armani jacket.

In certain circumstances, just wearing the right clothes can give you a feeling of strength. As I look at myself in the mirror, getting ready for a new kind of battle, I think, "I've got a lot to lose…but

I'm a fifty-five-year-old veteran who knows how to handle himself in the trenches." I have to believe it will all work out.

By the time I've had three or four meetings with my vendors, I can see that I'm not the first person to ever find himself in this situation. Some of them have their own horror stories to tell about near crashes their companies survived, and they're the ones who are most sympathetic to my situation.

With each conversation, I gain back some small part of my lost self-confidence as they reiterate their trust in me and ORLY. I begin to recognize my situation for what it is—a temporary setback that will eventually reverse itself and that this may even lead ORLY in a new and more profitable direction.

On the family front, I ask everyone to tighten their belt. Now everyone is on board and I'm ready to start this new chapter.

For the next two years, Veronica Reyes and I keep our noses to the grindstone, watching every penny and calculating the cost of every move. With the cooperation of our vendors, we continue receiving the manufacturing supplies necessary to keep ORLY in production. Slowly, slowly, we inch our way out of the red.

To show my appreciation, I give Veronica the title of CFO. It's not something I do lightly, unlike some companies that give out titles freely, often in lieu of better salaries. I've always believed that a title is something you had to earn. When someone is given a new title, they are expected to take on added responsibilities and receive increased compensation.

I actually had a situation where an employee asked for the title of vice president, even though they were unable to fulfill the requirements of the position. When I said I didn't think it was appropriate, the response was "I don't need a better salary, I just want the VP title so it will look good on my résumé." Needless to say, we parted ways shortly after that.

But with Veronica, it was a completely different story. She deserved the title. In fact, she was fulfilling the duties of chief financial officer even without the title. All I did was make it official.

12

GET A GRIP

It took us almost three years to dig ourselves out of a hole, but we did it and what was paramount was that ORLY never declared Chapter Eleven, which was against everything that I stood for. In 2000, I sat alone in the showroom of the ORLY headquarters in a nostalgic mood, surrounded by row-upon-row of colorful polishes, therapeutic nail creams, crystal clear topcoats—the products that were the output of my entire career. For me, every one of them had a story and collectively their stories made up the narrative of my business life.

As I looked around the showroom, once again I couldn't help thinking back to Jack Sperling's early advice about "finding the need," and to Abe Rosenbaum, whose experience and wisdom helped me create the Romeo Kit with the Nail Strengthener and Ridgefiller, the first two signature items that had launched ORLY and branded us as a company specializing in unique solutions for nail care.

It took a lot of courage in those early days to turn our backs on the popular focus of acrylics and artificial nails and to dedicate ourselves to developing innovative formulas for everyday nail problems. But we stuck to our guns and it paid off.

Across the room, my eyes rest on another gleaming display case; this one filled with the most significant item in our collection. Interestingly enough, it's not a treatment or nail care product…it's our famous fashion hit, The French Manicure.

By now, The French Manicure has become a highly-evolved concept with multiple versions of the "natural" colors and "white tips." We developed new ways to package it, new ways to apply it, and new "natural" colors that are variations on the original neutral polish and white tips. I still have a great sense of pride in the creation of The French Manicure and I think back to myself as a young man, bursting with enthusiasm and creative energy who gave birth to something that never existed before…something that had become a popular fashion concept worldwide.

Even though many attempts have been made to copy the idea, I take great pleasure in knowing that Jeff Pink will forever be credited as the originator of The French Manicure.

I look at the recently redesigned packaging and I'm reminded that several years after it was a worldwide success, we changed the name from "The French Manicure" to "The Original French Manicure." The reason we did it is an interesting story, one that taught me a very important business lesson.

When I first started ORLY, I was so deeply involved with every aspect of the business that sometimes things got away from me. You may recall that early in my career, I had forgotten to trademark the name ORLY, which cost me a bundle. I didn't see it as important and it wasn't a priority. Well, for some reason, I had also neglected to register the name 'The French Manicure."

Several years later, when The French Manicure was already very successful, my attorney went to apply for the trademark and he encountered a woman trademark officer who said, "You can't trademark that name; it's generic." I couldn't believe it. Something

I had created, something that never existed before, was now so generic that we couldn't trademark it. Our only recourse was to change the name to The Original French Manicure and to trademark that name.

To this day, I'm convinced that had that officer been a man, we would have gotten the trademark without question. Every woman knew about The French Manicure, but I doubt that many men did.

Even so, The French Manicure was the product that put us on the map and started the steady upward climb that took us from our humble beginnings in Jeff Pink's Beauty Supply to this 40,000-square-foot facility in Chatsworth.

Now, over twenty years later, here I am, sitting alone, surrounded by the output of a company that is slowly pulling back from the brink of disaster. I take a deep breath and give thanks that I've managed to turn the ship around.

I know that within a couple of years, all our creditors will be paid off and we'll be debt free. But I also know that for ORLY to thrive, it won't be enough just to regain our financial footing; it will take something new, some uniquely creative idea to achieve the prominence we previously enjoyed.

By now, I've had enough experience to know that new ideas cannot be forced into being. They come from deep within and have to be coaxed into existence. As I've done so many times before I ask myself a lot of questions. The first and most obvious question is, "How am I going to come up with a new idea?" It's a question that has no easy answer. Who knows where any new idea comes from? Or why the act of creativity is such an elusive process? And why it is that the harder you reach for it, the more it eludes you?

As I sit here pondering the very nature of creativity, the products call to me from the shelves, reminding me how each of them came to me through a gut instinct about something that was needed in the marketplace.

The Romeo was the first nail strengthener and the second was the Ridgefiller, and each helped solve the problem of weak and uneven nails. The Bonder, a special base coat made with rubber ingredients, prevented chipping. It became the number one basecoat in the professional market in the United States and remains so today. Nail Defense strengthened weak nails by using a protein base, and later, the Calcium Shield did the same for nails that responded better to a calcium base. Then for nails that required both the Ridgefiller and the Romeo, we came up with a new combination product called Nail Armor.

One by one, the need for new solutions brought about new products. In-A-Snap was a fast-drying topcoat. Top-To-Bottom was a base coat and a topcoat combined in one. Many of the treatment names were self-explanatory: Fungus MD, Won't Chip, No Bite, and Nails for Males, the first clear nail polish designed to provide a duller finish for men who didn't want it to be obvious they'd had a manicure.

Then, as I look around, I see our cuticle care line, which produced a big winner with Cuticle Therapy Crème, the product I had originally developed for my father's eczema, which had expanded into Cuticle Oil and Cuticle Care Complex.

On these shelves I can count over twenty-five unique items that ORLY has created, many of which have received special industry recognition. These awards got me through some hard times as reminders of our uniqueness in the industry. I think about the expression, "What has this person done in the past that will convince you that he can do what he says he can do." History can be a wonderful compass for where we are headed in the future. In 2001, something amazing occurred for ORLY. Annually, the

American Beauty Association presents the ABBIEs for achievement in marketing, innovation, and other categories. That year, ORLY was nominated for seven awards—unimaginable. The presentations took place at the iconic Breakers Hotel in Palm Beach, Florida. ORLY's representatives in both marketing and sales, along with myself, went there hoping to win one or two awards. When the winners were announced, we found out that we had received five of the seven awards for which we were nominated. Each of us went up to the stage to receive the awards. It was like winning five Academy Awards! We were more than elated to schlep the heavy metal back to Los Angeles, but when we got to the airport we were stopped by security because the airport was on high alert. It had only been three months earlier that the tragedy of the World Trade Center had occurred, so instead of carrying the awards on to the plane, we were required to pack them in our suitcases.

Now they are prominently displayed in our boardroom as a reminder of a momentous time in the growth of ORLY.

But you can't rest on your laurels.

We are already developing a new list of products to address other nail issues—products with names like Tough Cookie, Flash Dry, Nailtrition, Polishield, and Prime Time. There's no doubt in my mind that we will continue to be an innovator in the nail care industry, but the real question is: Will any one of these new products be groundbreaking enough to keep ORLY in a position of prominence?

My wheels begin to turn as I think about where the future lies. I know it's not in repeating history or doing more of the same. As usual, other companies are already copying my best ideas. What I need is a break-through product—something new that will make a real distinction between my competitors and me. Once again, it's time to think outside the box, time to think about the "need."

What are some of the common complaints that we hear in the nail care industry? Interestingly, one of the biggest complaints is not about the treatments or the colors; it's about the problems that both the professionals and the consumers have with opening the polish bottles.

Here's what happens: When you're applying the polish, a few drops always get onto the bottle threads and after several uses the bottle caps stick. It's difficult to get a grip on the hard-plastic bottle top because it's small and it slips around in your hand.

Just to get the bottles open, you have to struggle with pliers, rubber gloves, your teeth, or with running them under hot water or cold water, or banging them on tabletops. Sometimes you just have to abandon the bottle. It's been like that as long as there has been nail polish. Nobody has ever figured out a good way to deal with the problem. Once I have clearly identified a problem, magically, all the tumblers fall into place and I get a little click of an idea.

Every product I develop is for treating nails, but I never invented an application product. I say to myself, "Jeff, why don't you come up with something that will make it easier to open the bottle…like a special rubber cap that has a grip to it?"

Immediately, I know that I have hit on something that could resolve a big problem for manicurists and consumers. I've found a "need."

The name comes to me instantaneously. I call it "The Gripper Cap" and with a rush of excitement that I haven't had in years, I am off and running on to my next big adventure.

Having learned my lesson well, I start the application for the patent while we are still in the early stages of development. I know it will take time for the patent to be granted but it will also take time to develop this new cap and I want it to be protected when we bring it into the market.

Fortunately, I know just the man to help me develop my idea. His name is Roland Baranes. He's a major supplier of the glass bottles and hard plastic caps that I purchase. I know he's also a creative thinker and enjoys a challenge. Roland is based in Milan, so I fly there and meet him at the Armani Restaurant.

We sit on their outdoor patio bathed in the kind of dappled light you only find in Italy. Over a cappuccino and an incredible cannoli, I tell him about my idea for the Gripper Cap.

"It has to be a combination of a hard plastic inside and rubber on the outside, and I want you to help me develop it. Why don't we work together on this?" Roland is flattered. He loves the idea and our collaboration begins.

The biggest challenge is coming up with a way to combine two different substances that do not easily go together. It means working with new materials and creating a special kind of production mold that neither of us had done before. It takes almost a year to develop, but we are both up to the challenge and I know Roland will make it work.

It's already 2002, and while Roland is in the final stages of development, I begin working on what will prove to be the most effective advertising campaign in the history of ORLY. I already know that the concept of the Gripper Cap will be mind-blowing to the nail industry and I want to launch it in a mind-blowing way.

By now ORLY is on solid financial footing. I'm able to pay off my creditors a full year earlier than I had committed to. It's time to start adding back more staff. Soon enough, we have our own in-house advertising team once again.

I know from past experience how important it is when launching something new to spend money on advertising and I know exactly how I want to launch the Gripper Cap—with teaser ads.

The whole idea of the teaser ad is to stimulate interest and curiosity without revealing exactly what it is you're doing or why you're doing it. I sit down with my marketing team and we come up with an ad campaign that is every bit as exciting as the Gripper Cap.

The campaign is designed to run in trade magazines that are read by manicurists and retailers. We run the first ad about six months before we're ready to launch the Gripper Cap. The ad has a picture of sunglasses and the text reads, "Sunglasses were invented in 1931," and at the bottom it says, "ORLY...to be continued." People read that and say "Sunglasses? What do sunglasses have to do with ORLY?"

Then a month later, the next advertisement shows a zipper. "The Zipper. Invented in 1929. Yet to come...ORLY." Then over the next few months we run ads that show a whole series of different inventions over the years including the bikini and hair spray.

Readers are curious; they don't know what ORLY is up to, but they are intrigued. Anytime they ask we say, "Wait, you'll see." Then finally we run a picture of a bottle of red nail polish with our newly designed cap. The text reads, "The Gripper Cap...invented in 2002, by ORLY."

When we finally reveal the product, people say, "Wow!" They're blown away! The Gripper Cap is an instant hit through the magic of teaser ads that build up to the final reveal.

With the success of The Gripper Cap, inevitably other manufacturers try to copy it, but we have a fully-secured patent protecting our invention, and nobody but ORLY can manufacture a rubberized cap. Orders go through the roof and The Gripper Cap puts ORLY back on the map. Big time.

One of the steps I take during the long period of recovery is to define a "culture of ORLY," which is designed to draw everyone together into a common way of thinking about the importance of shared values.

I don't want ORLY to be a collection of different departments, each isolated in their own little world. I want us to operate as a single entity in which every person at every level has respect for everyone else in the company and is willing to help anyone who asks for it. No matter if they're from another department or if they do a different job. We should all feel part of the same team and share the same pride in our work.

I especially want a calm and clean environment. If anyone, from a vice president to an assembly line worker, sees trash on the floor, they pick it up. It isn't left for someone else to do. I also have very little tolerance for office drama or loud, disruptive arguing, and I believe that honest differences can be settled with open communication and discussion. People who want to hold grudges or badmouth their fellow workers don't belong at ORLY.

If there is one word that sums up what I feel is the most important attribute for being part of the ORLY team, it is RESPECT. And the importance of that word cannot be overstated: respect for ORLY and respect for one another.

In a recent study, it was shown that when given a choice between what people want most, respect came out ahead of power and fame. Respect makes you walk tall and hold your head high. And who doesn't like to live or work in an atmosphere that promotes that kind of well-being?

There are a lot of moving parts to reinforce the "ORLY culture." One of my favorites is the group outings we hold for our employees and their families. We go to recreation parks, play baseball and eat hot dogs and hamburgers. We have holiday parties and an annual cookout where we set up big barbecues in the headquarters' parking lot and I, along with the other top executives, put on aprons and chef hats and cook lunch for more than two hundred employees.

But the very best thing I came up with was a decision to have one-on-one meetings with all the management and middle-management staff every year.

This isn't so much for my benefit as it is for theirs. How often does an employee get invited to come to the corporate office, to sit down with the boss and have a casual conversation about their personal life, their spouse and family, and get asked if they have any questions or suggestions about how their work is going?

It's hard to say exactly what that does for an employee, but I like to think that when that person goes home and tells the family how they sat down with the boss today and had a pleasant conversation, that he or she is elevated not only in the eyes of their loved ones but in their own eyes as well.

As a result, that employee rewards you with the kind of devotion and loyalty that money can't buy. Again, it's just a matter of showing respect.

Within two years of the creation of the Gripper Cap, the company has become so successful that once again we run out of space. It's time to make another big move only this one will be very different. In the past, we always rented our facilities. This time I am determined to own the building instead of leasing.

We start the search for a suitable building, and in 2004, I find a great property in Van Nuys. It was formerly a TV production facility owned by Fonovisa, and the floor plan was divided into small offices and studios for filming and recording. These are of no use to us and we know right away that we're going to gut the entire building and start from scratch. The only thing that we decide to keep is a small screening room. I know we can make use of that. The educational component of ORLY is growing and having our own screening room where we can show videos about ORLY's latest products to our distributors and customers will be very useful. It's also very classy.

With the help of architect Karen Fisher, we turn the building into a multipurpose headquarters to house the corporate offices of ORLY, the manufacturing space, and the shipping warehouse.

Karen's design for the corporate offices brings that extra feminine touch of lushness and sensitivity. It's bright and airy and filled with beautiful graphics drawn from the archives of our past ad campaigns. She designs an entryway through an impressive glass façade into a high-ceiling reception area where, behind a sleek modern desk, hangs a delicate chain link curtain that bears the "O" from the ORLY name, and on the floor is a large hand-woven carpet with the same signature "O." The design says everything I want it to communicate: that ORLY is efficient, artistic and thriving. My vision is that when someone steps through those glass doors, they immediately know that ORLY strives to be the best.

In 2005, on the day of our official opening, I stand on the steps of our new headquarters, surrounded by my co-workers, my children, and my colleagues—including my life-long friend, Jack Sperling.

I think about how far I've come from that first opening of Jeff Pink's Beauty Supply in that little mall storefront in Tarzana, to this beautiful ten-million-dollar facility—an investment that we are able to afford by virtue of a lot of hard work, creativity, and commitment. My sense of gratitude to all the people who have helped me along the way is overwhelming. We pop the champagne corks and drink to the future.

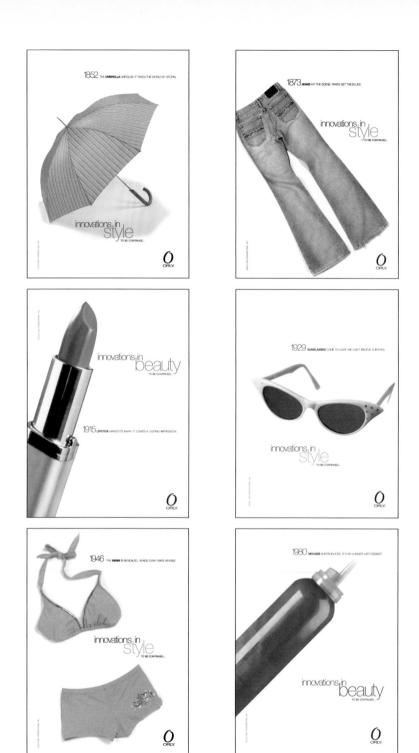

The Gripper Cap teaser ad campaign, 2002.

104

The Gripper Cap teaser ad campaign, 2002.

Twelve ABBIE Awards won by ORLY, 1998–2003.

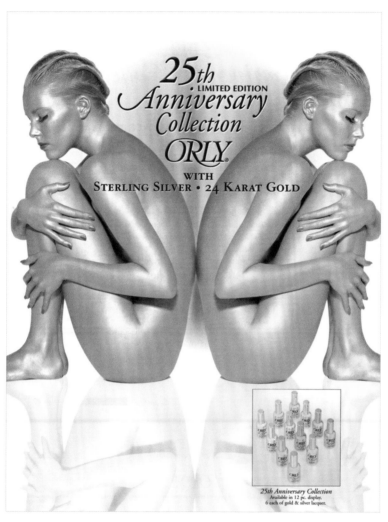

The Silver and Gold Nail Polish Collection in honor of ORLY's
25th Anniversary, 2000.

13

THE PRICE OF SUCCESS

It's 6:00 p.m. on a Friday evening. Almost everyone has gone home except Veronica Reyes and me. Veronica's unwavering dedication to ORLY over these past fourteen years has earned her the title of VP of Finance and Human Resources. I'm ready to head out but seeing Veronica hunched over her desk, still deeply engrossed in her work makes me stop. "Veronica, that's enough. Whatever it is can wait until Monday. Go on home."

She barely looks up. "No, Jeff. This has to go out today. It's that company in Texas. They're already three months late on the payment for our last shipment. You go ahead, I'll lock up. I just need to make sure this gets taken care of tonight."

There's no arguing with Veronica. She feels that she carries the weight of the entire company on her shoulders. She can't quite get used to the fact that ORLY has pulled out of the nosedive and is steadily returning to the profitable company we once were. I know it can be hard to change gears after such a long uphill climb, and I'm grateful for her devotion to ORLY, but I think that Veronica, like me, needs a little break.

That night I'm having dinner with Steve Wasserman. It's something we do on a regular basis. We always try to go someplace special and tonight we're enjoying a prime rib dinner cooked to perfection. It's nice to sit down with a good friend, some great food, and stimulating conversation. This is one of the reasons I work so hard…so that I can enjoy the good things in life.

Steve is very complimentary about the way things have gone for ORLY. "It's truly amazing, Jeff. How you turned ORLY around."

I nod. "Thank God."

"So, what's next?" he asks. Steve can read my mind.

"You know, Steve, that's exactly what I've been thinking about…what's the next step…how do we build on all this success."

Steve looks at me with satisfaction. "It sounds like you're ready to restructure." I know exactly what he means. It's the well-known curse of business that if you don't keep growing you begin to stagnate. It's time for ORLY to make another big move. This time it's not to a larger space; it's to a larger corporate structure.

We've already begun making small-scale changes by taking on new staff in the marketing department, but now it's time to bring in some big guns—executives who are established professionals, people who can streamline our operations and move us to the next level. Most importantly, we need additional executives who can take the day-to-day burden off Veronica and me. I know this is our next big challenge.

I think about it all weekend. Monday morning, I'm fired up about bringing in new upper management staff and ready to get started.

I'm eager to discuss my ideas with Veronica. We have a morning meeting scheduled and she shows up waving our latest financial report. Veronica is in love with numbers and she points proudly to a graph that climbs steadily upwards. "Look at this, Jeff. This is where we were in 2007, just a year ago, and this is where we are now. That's a ten percent growth in profits."

She has a right to be proud. "This is wonderful, Veronica. And that's exactly what I want to talk to you about." She looks at me brightly like a student that's just been patted on the head. "Yes," she says, eager for me to go on.

"Veronica, I think we're finally at a point where we can afford to bring in some additional personnel to take the burden off our shoulders."

Her look changes to puzzlement. "What kind of help?" I sense a tone of concern in her voice so I proceed with caution.

"Veronica, you and I have been carrying a heavy load for a long time and there's no doubt that the two of us have done a great job. The numbers prove that. But I think the time is right to spread some of the responsibility around."

I see her back stiffen. "To whom?"

I'm a little surprised at her reaction; I thought she would welcome the idea. I find myself back pedaling, "I don't know yet exactly who. I just think it's time to start looking."

Veronica gathers up her reports without looking at me, "It's your company, Jeff. You can do whatever you want, but I thought we were a pretty good team."

She leaves and I can sense that a deep seismic shift has taken place.

This is where things get hard. My loyalty to Veronica is limitless. It's the kind of bond you form with someone you've struggled side-by-side with through the hard times. You share the same war stories; you bear the same scars; and you revel in the same triumphs. You never forget those relationships; they become part of who you are and you never take them for granted. But ORLY has to keep growing and that requires making changes.

Veronica has worked successfully in a certain way for the past fourteen years. It may be hard for her to accept change. Only time will tell. Without her blessing, I make the decision to search for new personnel. I pray that she'll come around and be part of the future of ORLY.

I begin the search for a head of marketing, and in 2009, we identify and hire an amazing woman, Carina Breda, who's at Procter & Gamble Corporation and was previously at Wella AG, the German-based hair products company. I've always liked to employ people who know more than I do, and Carina is definitely one of those people. Carina knows the beauty business and she knows how to operate in the corporate world. She's half-German and half-Italian and her personality combines the best of those two cultures: in business she's no-nonsense, very practical and straightforward, and yet she has flamboyance and warmth. Her experience and qualifications are exactly what I'm looking for and I can see right away how her creative thinking is going to help change ORLY.

I have already found a Vice President of Operations, Bill Korn, who had worked at Unilever, a multi-national company in the consumer products industry. Bill starts right away by streamlining our operations: production, inventory, shipping, receiving, purchasing, and the warehouse all come under his scrutiny. He quickly raises our overall efficiency while never losing the human touch—just the way we like to operate at ORLY.

Our two other major hires are Dan Shorts, who will be the Vice President of North American Sales, and Bob Hobe, Vice President of International Sales. By the end of 2009, I have a great team—including these four new hires—in place and I'm ready to start making some bold moves. That's a lot of star power to absorb into the ORLY culture, but it's exciting for me to see how all these talented professionals will coalesce.

Throughout it all, Veronica has kept pretty quiet, hunkering down even further into her work. I continue to express my optimism that she'll see how much the new hires have to offer and that she'll show interest in what they bring to the company's potential for growth.

Carina spends a couple of months learning how the company operates. The first thing she recommends is that we invest $100,000 in a market research study to find out exactly what people think about ORLY and where we stand in the world of nail care businesses. Carina makes a good case, "Jeff, you need to learn about your customers; what drives them and what motivates them to buy. We need to analyze the brand perceptions of ORLY; what people think when they hear the name. That's how we'll be able to define a new brand image and a strategy for ORLY to be a real competitor."

I think it's a good idea because "knowledge is power." I agree to her plan but when Carina asks to see a copy of our current 2009 budget, I'm embarrassed to admit that we've never had one. She assures me that a budget is an absolute necessity for any company, however large or small. "It gives a company a road map on how to achieve specific goals."

She's right and this is exactly what I've hired her for, to help expand the vision of ORLY and to put systems in place that will help us manage ORLY's growth. I like what she has to say, and I arrange for her to meet with Veronica, who has all of ORLY'S financial information.

A few weeks later, Carina brings in a market research company to make a presentation. At the meeting, they lay out a plan that has specific goals and they explain how their test groups will reveal what people think about ORLY and how we are perceived by the general public. Based on what they learn from that research, they will advise us on how to help shape the future of ORLY. It sounds like a good approach and we shake on a deal.

After the consultants leave, Carina says, "By the way, Jeff, do you think you could speak to Veronica about the financial information I asked for? It's been over a month and I've asked her twice." I apologize and promise to talk with Veronica.

Later that afternoon, I go to Veronica's office where she's intently focused on a ledger book. Her shell-framed glasses are balanced on the tip of her nose and when she sees me, she pushes them back into place.

"Oh, hi, Jeff. You need something?"

"Veronica, I see you're busy. I don't want to interrupt. I just wanted to ask you to please give Carina the financial documents she requested."

Veronica sticks a post-it in the ledger to mark her place and shuts the book. She looks at me very protectively, "Jeff, I can't do that. It's not right."

"I don't understand, Veronica. What's not right?"

She looks away, shaking her head. "Giving out our financial information to anyone who wants it. That's private company information. Nobody needs to know that, just you and me."

I pull up a chair and sit down across from her. "Veronica, I think you and I need to have a discussion."

For the next twenty minutes, I try to make her understand that the company is operating in a new way and that it requires us to be flexible, to change the way we do things.

"It's not just the two of us anymore, Veronica. It's Carina and Dan and Bob and Bill—they're our partners now and we need to be transparent with them. They all need to know about our finances because they are going to be involved in how the company is run in the future. They can't do their jobs without critical financial information."

No matter what I say, Veronica keeps insisting that I'm making a big mistake. I end up pleading with her. She makes a valiant promise to try, but my gut feeling is that it's not going to work out.

14

TELL IT LIKE IT IS

In the spring of 2010, I'm in my office going over the colors for the next season's nail polish collection. The range of colors runs from blue to purple and orange to red. Every company comes up with their own interpretation of those colors based on what they believe their consumers are likely to go for and then we create our new collection to match those colors.

I had just painted a sample of our new electric blue on my pinkie fingernail when my executive assistant, Shaina Martin, buzzes me. Shaina is a new hire who came to ORLY after working with some famous attorneys. I could see right away that Shaina possessed that incredible female quality of bringing order out of chaos. Within weeks, she had taken my office and organized it completely. As an added bonus, she's a joy to be around because she has a wonderful sense of humor.

I pick up the phone and Shaina says, "Jeff, guess what? *The Wall Street Journal* is on the line…"

"What do they want?" I ask.

Shaina chuckles, "I think they want you to do some kind of a talk!"

As flattering as it is, I'm not crazy about making speeches. As much as I love to talk about ORLY, I'm a little shy on the public stage. My English isn't always perfect, and I prefer to talk one on one. But the woman on the phone is very convincing; she assures me that I will not be speaking alone. I'll be part of a panel made up of five successful entrepreneurs.

She explains that *The Journal* is holding a round-table discussion in Atlanta, Georgia, for an audience of young businesspeople who are interested in starting their own companies. The other panelists and I will all be sharing the stage and I'll only have to talk about my personal experience and whatever strategies I think were essential to my success. The title of the panel is, "How I Built It." Okay, that I know I can do; I accept her invitation.

Right away my head starts spinning about what I can say to this group of eager, young business hopefuls who are paying good money to hear from the "experts." I ask myself, "What have I learned that is worth passing on?" In the end, I decide that the most important thing I can share with them are some of the hard lessons I've learned through success and failure. I don't want to sugarcoat what ORLY has been through, but rather give them an honest portrayal of the highs and lows and tell them what it takes to survive and thrive, how it's critically important to constantly reassess what you are doing to innovate. "Same old, same old" doesn't cut it in the beauty business, or in any business for that matter.

On September 16, 2010. I fly to Atlanta. It's a typically muggy Fall day in Georgia, but *The Wall Street Journal* knows how to do things right. They put me up in the luxurious St. Regis Hotel along with all the other panelists. That evening, we all meet in the elegant white-marbled lobby under a massive crystal chandelier that speaks of the early grandeur of the South. We are taken to dinner in a private dining room in the hotel's famed Atlas Buckhead Restaurant where we are surrounded by an impressive collection of art by van Gogh, Picasso, and Chagall.

I meet the other panelists and notice right away they are considerably younger than me. For the most part, their newly-formed companies are information-based technology companies. The moderator of the panel will be Colleen DeBaise, the small business editor of *The Wall Street Journal*. It's a lively and intelligent group and the panel promises to be very interesting.

The next morning, we all file into a large meeting room filled with round dining tables where the two hundred attendees are being served a lavish breakfast. After breakfast, the panelists are announced and one by one we climb to the stage to speak about our companies. The audience is attentive and serious. They're hanging on our every word.

I listen with great interest to the other four panelists who are all part of the new generation of Internet technology success stories. Each of them has an inspiring tale of how they came up with an idea in their dorm room or their parents' basement and how they followed their dream even when people told them it couldn't be done.

I'm sure that their messages resonate with many of the young people in the audience. But I'm the one on the panel who has a "brick and mortar" company, who has built something with my own two hands from the ground up, who has taken the roller coaster ride to the very top and all the way back down again.

When my turn comes to make introductory remarks, I'm identified as the founder and CEO of ORLY and the creator of the Original French Manicure. I look out at the sea of enthusiastic faces. I know they are hoping for some uplifting and encouraging message, but I feel a deep obligation to avoid any kind of superficiality. I decide to give it to them straight. Here's what I say:

"You've heard some exceptional stories here today about what it's like to create a start-up company and become a 'big success.' But what I'd like to talk to you about is how you measure success when you've run a company for over thirty-five years, when you've navigated some very rough waters and come out still standing strong and successful.

"The big question that is always on the mind of every CEO is 'Where do we stand in relation to our competition?' Becoming number one is part of the American dream and for many years at ORLY we were number one. But one of the truths we all have to accept in life, and in business, is that nothing lasts forever, including your status as number one.

"When I started ORLY, it was a heyday for the nail industry and I hit the wave at exactly the right moment. It was a time when women were moving into the workplace and luxuries like manicures and pedicures were no longer an extravagance, they were a necessity. This not only greatly increased the sales of existing nail products; it opened up opportunities for new innovations in the nail care industry.

"That was where ORLY held the number one spot from 1980 to 1998; no one else was coming up with creative ideas that could match ours. We were at the top of our game and it felt like our success would go on forever. And that's where our problem started.

"Because I was convinced that ORLY was on a never-ending climb to the top, I decided to move overseas and develop the international market. I was not aware that my absence would leave a vacuum that would slowly but surely be filled by other companies. But that's exactly what happened. When ORLY's place as number one was threatened, all we could think of was how to hold on to it.

"We decided that one of the ways to maintain our dominance was to change our direction. For years we had focused on creating products for the professional nail care market. Now we decided to do something new; to go head-to-head with our competition in the consumer market. That was our next crucial mistake.

"We had very little experience in that field and we were desperate to do something bold in order to preserve our status. Desperation can drive you to make mistakes and that's exactly what happened. Our venture into the consumer market was a financial disaster and we almost lost the company.

"I completely blame myself for this. I took the time off and walked away from the company that I built from the ground up. I took my eye off the ball and trusted that other people could do what I did. What I learned from this experience was that the greatest danger in success is complacency and that business is not static; it's a game that's in constant motion and you have to stay focused on which way the winds of change are blowing.

"Once we recovered from our brush with near disaster, I promised myself that rather than chasing after some elusive symbol of success, I would dedicate myself to creating a company that stood for something of lasting value.

"At some point, I had to acknowledge that maybe ORLY might never be number one again, but we would always be recognized as the industry leader in quality and innovation. And that's exactly what we have done for thirty-five years. That, to me, is what I call a 'big success.'"

When I finish speaking, the audience gives me an enthusiastic round of applause. After my presentation, I am deluged with questions. Everyone wants to know more about the difficulties I had faced and how I had overcome them. It's gratifying to see that what I had gone through in my thirty-five-year career is of interest to these young entrepreneurs.

At the end of the conference, the moderator from the *Wall Street Journal* takes me aside and says, "Jeff, you have such a great story…you ought to write a book. It would be inspirational and informative."

I smile and say, "Maybe one day."

Jeff Pink with other presenters at the *Wall Street Journal*
Roundtable for the "How I Built It" panel,
Atlanta, Georgia, 2010.

All presenters with moderator, Colleen DeBaise (far right),

Shaina Martin, my "right hand" executive assistant, who kept me organized and strived to always stay a step ahead of me. Her presence added clout and respect to the executive office. (Pictured here with Max, her beloved Mastiff.)

15

OLD WINE, NEW BOTTLE

In early 2011, the results are in from the market research. I sit down with Carina, her staff, and the research guys to analyze the data. It's like a doctor examining an X-ray. All the signs point to the fact that ORLY is "suffering from an aging image." People think of us as a brand that's been around for a long time.

According to the research, the big creative, open letter "O" that dominates all our packaging is seen as "optimistic, playful and trustworthy," but our promotions and website are judged as having "too much going on, that we're undecided and have no common visual language."

The report goes on to say that the name ORLY is associated with quality products, but the name doesn't evoke any feeling of excitement or relevance to today's market trends.

We immediately swing into action. Carina brings in a company that specializes in branding. It's not the first time we've made a big change. The ORLY logo has been redesigned three times over in the past forty years, each time becoming more attuned to the times. But now it will be more than just updating our logo; we need to change our packaging and the look of all our products.

We need what is commonly known in the beauty world as a "complete makeover."

This can't happen overnight. It will take a couple of years to redesign the packaging and create a completely new image for ORLY, but our team is eager to take on the challenge.

For me, this is an exciting time because this is where creativity and business meet. There is a deep connection between the world of art and business, at least in my industry, and perhaps in many others. I believe that anytime you are involved with the creation of something new, you need to draw upon your intuitive, artistic sensibilities.

Working with your architect, or your graphic designers, or deciding the shape of a new bottle—all of these require an understanding of color, shape, form, and of the dynamics of tempo and rhythm, especially if you're working in the beauty industry. I never had formal art training, but I know from my years of listening to all kinds of music, appreciating sculptures and paintings, and honing my own personal artistic tastes have helped me enormously in business.

When I sit down with our marketing people, our graphic designers and our copywriters to come up with a new image for ORLY, we're not just a collection of thinkers in search of a concept, we're a team of artists working together, all heading toward a common goal: to create a new and exciting image for the ORLY brand. All that matters is that we get it right! It takes patience and effort. It takes reshaping, rethinking, and endless tweaking to get it where we want.

The logo design we come up with is much bolder than our old design. It incorporates the entire name ORLY, preceded by a signature "color swatch." Our website and advertising feature a lot of open white space and are easy to read and less cluttered. The photographic style is modernized as well as the product containers, packaging, and in-store modular displays.

The rebranding of the company is a shot in the arm for almost everyone in the company and signals the start of a new era for ORLY. There's a palpable feeling of excitement about our future, but unfortunately, it's a future that doesn't include someone who has been with me for over fifteen years.

For the past two years, Veronica Reyes and I have had continuing disagreements about the management style of ORLY. She's done her best to adjust and adapt to the changes taking place, but to no avail.

In 2012, we both know that it's over. It's one of the saddest days of my career. Separating from Veronica is like cutting an umbilical cord. The decision to move on without her is traumatic for me, but there are two hundred other employees who are depending on me to stay on track.

What I want most is to make sure that Veronica is financially secure. She's a single mother raising a son on her own. I give her a generous severance package and promise that when I sell the company, Veronica will receive a percentage of the sale. I know it won't soften the blow of leaving, but at least it's a reminder of how much she has meant to me and to ORLY.

Veronica does not want a special good-bye party. She's a very private person and only wants to thank her staff and leave. Fortunately, because of her dedication to detail, she leaves the financial records in complete order and everything is ready for her successor to take over seamlessly. Furthermore, Veronica's successor praised her for leaving behind a great team in her department.

The night of Veronica's departure, I leave ORLY headquarters with a heavy heart. I take a last glimpse around my office at all the new campaign artwork and I can see how everything we've invested our time and our energy into for the past two years is finally coming together. It promises to be a major shot in the arm for ORLY. I know I should be feeling excited and grateful, but the loss of Veronica has left me with a deep feeling of sadness.

Several months later, I'm crossing the nearly empty parking lot one evening and I see Kanisha Muslar, from our Customer Care department, walking toward the bus stop. Kanisha came to us as a temporary replacement for our front desk receptionist on maternity leave. She had no previous work experience, but she was so good at dealing with people that I asked ORLY's Director of Customer Care, Letty Marin, to see if she could find her a position in her department when our regular receptionist returned. Letty agreed and together we interviewed Kanisha and hired her as a Customer Care Specialist and full-time employee of ORLY.

Today, as I get into my car, I make a mental note to ask why she's taking the bus. The next morning as I enter ORLY, I see Kanisha who greets me with her friendly smile. "Good morning, Mr. Pink!"

Suddenly I remember my promise to talk to her. "Kanisha, come into my office. I want to speak to you about something."

Her dark eyes dart in surprise and her brow furrows, "Is there a problem, Mr. Pink?"

"No, no problem, I just have a question for you."

She sits across from my big desk looking a little tense. I don't have to start the conversation by complimenting her; there's no criticism coming. I just want to know why she's taking the bus instead of driving to work. Her answer is simple; she can't afford a car.

Then I learn that she's got an hour bus ride to and from work every day. I still have that same opinion about people living no more than thirty to forty-five minutes from where they work. I decide to make her an offer. "Kanisha, what do you think about ORLY buying you a car and you can pay us back little by little."

An incredulous smile lights her face, "Really, Mr. Pink?"

"Yes, really," I say. "It's not the first time I've done it. Sometimes when we have a good employee who needs a car, we find a way to help out."

"That would be awesome, Mr. Pink. I think my grandmother would help me get insurance and what I'll save on bus fare will help pay for gas."

Kanisha is ecstatic. She gives me a big "thank you" hug and practically floats out of my office on a cloud of joy. I think back to the car I helped buy for Glen, ORLY's maintenance man, so many years ago and how doing a small kindness for an employee can have enormous returns. I'm happy to do this for Kanisha. Actually, it gives me a real kick. I'm still agonizing over the loss of Veronica Reyes and it's made me very aware of how we strive to do good things at ORLY. I try even harder to make sure that we care about one another and that everybody does what they can do to help each other out...and that includes me.

A few weeks later as I'm leaving work, a bright voice calls out to me across the parking lot. "Mr. Pink!" I look up and see Kanisha standing by her car. She points to it and gives me a big smile and two thumbs up, "Thank you, Mr. Pink. You're the best."

I nod and smile back. Seated behind my steering wheel I stop for a moment, take a deep breath, and say to myself, "Thank you, Kanisha. You don't know how much I appreciate that."

By the time we're ready to roll out the new branding, it's 2013. It's taken great patience and great care to make sure that everything has been done properly. We're just about to finalize the campaign when Carina and her staff make a surprising proposal.

We're at a meeting in my office where I'm set to give my final stamp of approval on all the packaging and advertising when Carina says, "Jeff, there's one more thing we'd like to do. We've all given this idea a lot of thought and we hope you'll agree. As part of the new image for ORLY, we think we should use an image of you in all the new company branding."

It's a shocking idea and I'm not comfortable with it. I immediately reject it. I shake my head vehemently, "No, I've seen some of my contemporaries use their own photos in ad campaigns and it always strikes me as self-serving. The public doesn't care what you look like. It's your products that count. It's ORLY that should shine, not Jeff Pink." I'm adamant about it but Carina won't give up easily.

She says, "Okay, Jeff, let me see what I can come up with."

A few weeks later, she presents me with a possible solution. In Paris, she's found an artist, Françoise Nielly, who does modern abstract paintings of people's faces. She shows me a sample of the artist's work—a painting of Sylvester Stallone. It's a construction of shapes and colors that are not a realistic representation of Stallone, yet his identity and personality shine through.

I have to admire Carina's tenacity and the brilliance of this artist. I study the painting for a few minutes while Carina softly drums her fingers in anticipation. "Well, what do you think, Jeff?" Slowly I look up at her and nod my head, "Yes, that I could agree to do."

A few weeks later, I am on a plane to Paris where I will meet with the artist, Françoise Nielly. She brings me to her studio and shoots a lot of photographs of my face. We talk at length about my work, especially about my nail colors. She tells me, "I'll have something to show you in two or three weeks," and I'm on my way back to Los Angeles.

Two weeks later, I receive the results. The portrait is astonishing. Françoise Nielly has taken the palette of our nail colors and used the actual polishes to create an abstract of my photo that perfectly embodies both my image and the image of ORLY. Everyone loves it and it becomes the signature of our advertising campaign accompanied by the text: "IT ALL STARTED WITH PINK."

It will take six months to prepare the campaign for delivery to the magazines and they need the visuals and the copy three months in advance of the next issue. It will be almost a year from the time it was conceived, but it's looking really outstanding. Then we make another big decision. Instead of running only in the trade magazines as we usually do, we buy ads in *COSMOPOLITAN, PEOPLE, GLAMOUR,* and other popular glossies.

More than 9.6 million women read *INSTYLE* magazine each month, so we purchase a special edition of the magazine which has a separate wrap over the regular cover that features our campaign, "IT ALL STARTED WITH PINK." *INSTYLE* magazine prints 100,000 copies of our special salon edition and as soon as we launch the campaign, we send them out to major salons all over the country.

This is all part of our carefully orchestrated plan to expand consumer awareness of ORLY and we're keeping our fingers crossed that it will work.

Jeff Pink with artist Françoise Nielly at her atelier in
Paris, France. February 2013.

Jeff Pink with Françoise Nielly and her team in
Paris, France. February 2013.

IT ALL STARTED WITH PINK advertising campaign in 2013.

16

GLOBAL GLAMOUR IN L.A.

For many years, ORLY has held a prominent place in the international market for beauty products. Our valued distributors are from all over the world and we celebrate their contributions with an International Conference which takes place on a somewhat regular basis. Since 2005, we have held conferences in such diverse places as Slovakia, Turkey, Spain, Thailand, and Croatia. We try to give people an unusual and enjoyable experience.

In September 2013, the conference takes place in Los Angeles for the first time. It's a glamorous event held at the Sheraton Universal Hotel right next to Universal Studios and Hollywood. On arrival, the 144 guests are greeted by sixty flags decorating the hotel entrance, representing each of their countries.

The conference schedule is jam-packed with three days of information sharing and education, but in addition to the all-important business, there's time to enjoy a tour of Universal Studios and a visit to the ORLY headquarters in Van Nuys.

The real heart of the conference centers around three main topics: introducing our upcoming branding of ORLY's new products and packaging, educating our distributors about our complete ORLY line, and information sharing among the distributors about how they promote and advertise ORLY in their countries.

Everyone is eager to see the new collections, so that's how we start the conference. It's also the perfect time to introduce our 2013 branding by unveiling the Françoise Nielly portrait and rolling out the new slogan "It All Started With Pink." We screen a video portrait created by my daughter, Shanee, chronicling my early career and the origins of the ORLY brand. Later, at dinner, we all raise a toast with a special "Pink-mopolitan" cocktail created just for the event. The conference may be about business, but we like to have fun along the way.

Our Education Department sets up workshops led by Catherine Baek, ORLY's Head of Education, and ORLY's Ambassadors/Educators who dispense the kind of inside information that will help everyone understand exactly how the products are designed to be used and how to talk to their customers about the new developments in the ORLY line. But the most enjoyable part of the conference is when the distributors show videos and describe how they build customer relations through personal events and advertisements geared towards their specific country's markets. It's always inspiring to the other distributors and generates a lot of discussion about what worked well and what didn't work so well. It can even get emotional with stories about overcoming great adversity or achieving some exceptional results.

By the end of the conference, these shared human stories always bring the group closer together and friendships are formed that last for years.

A lot of thoughts about the changing nature of the business are running through my mind as I prepare for tonight's big dinner at the international conference. One hundred and forty-four distributors will be there. Some I know very well…some I've never met. I have to make a speech but I'm still not sure what I'm going to say. In the afternoon, we take a group of distributors on a tour of the ORLY headquarters. We start in the "Trophy Room" where all our awards and accolades are on display and then move on to the ORLY Museum where the history, memorabilia, and original products from the early '60s are exhibited. Elsbeth Schutz is on the tour. She has been with the company for twenty-three years helping me to put ORLY on the international map, spreading the nail category as an important part of the beauty industry, which, in the beginning, was really in its infancy. Over the years, she has trained other Ambassadors/Educators and traveled along with Nadia Deering, Vice President of International Sales, introducing our distributors to ORLY's newest products, dynamically demonstrating how to use them and what to tell our distributors in order to sell them. She has been an invaluable member of the ORLY team. Due to our special relationship, she insisted on writing a few words for this memoir about me:

"He [Jeff Pink] is fearless and bold and sharp and stylish and funny and has shown it ever since we opened up Russia and Eastern Europe for ORLY in '96. He was able to attract so many people in this new-to-the-world nail market that people traveled hundreds of miles to attend our seminars. It was such a success—as were most of our trips."

While on our tour of ORLY, Elsbeth asks me, "Jeff, when you first started ORLY, did you have any idea that it would become this big?"

I shake my head. "The truth is, I never thought about it. All I was thinking about was how to pay the rent and put food on the table."

Elsbeth laughs and says, "What's your secret, Jeff? How did it happen?"

I stop and think about that for a minute. "You know, Elsbeth, that's a very good question and when you come to the dinner tonight, I think you'll hear the answer." I go back to my office and start making some notes for my speech.

At 7:00 p.m., we arrive at the ballroom on the top floor of the Universal Sheraton overlooking a commanding view of Los Angeles and the river of freeways that tie the sprawling city together. The ballroom is glowing with candlelight and sparkling crystal as the crowd begins to filter in. Sprinkled among the guests are members of the staff, some of my closest friends, Orly Pink, and my children, Ran, Tal, and Shanee Pink.

On one side of the stage, a trio of musicians provides an up-tempo background to the lively chatter of people who've come to have a good time. Everyone is dressed to perfection. Many of the women have been to an afternoon nail design workshop where they've had their nails done with incredible patterns and colors to match their outfits.

A banner featuring the ORLY logo dominates the stage, and on every table is a beautifully designed centerpiece built around bottles of silver and gold polish clustered together like a bouquet of flowers. Cindy Cebulak, ORLY's event and tradeshow manager, has outdone herself. She always gives 100 percent to everything she does, and her enthusiasm and attention to detail are what makes this celebration so spectacular.

The "Pink-mopolitans" flow freely and a delicious dinner is served. After dinner, we present our Awards of Excellence. This has become a traditional part of the conference where we recognize individual distributors for their outstanding performance in marketing, consumer sales, and professional development. It's one of the many ways that we thank our great teams from all over the world. Then it's time for my speech. I enter the stage and look out at a sea of smiling faces. This is my extended family and I want them to know that I have a sense of responsibility towards them, that I still feel that same obligation "to pay the rent and put food on the table," not just for my immediate family but also for the hundreds of ORLY employees and affiliates around the world.

I've made some notes on 3x5 cards, which I take out of my pocket, but I don't really need them because what I have to say comes from my heart. I step up to the microphone and the ballroom goes quiet:

"One of the biggest misconceptions about business is that once you've 'made it,' you can sit back and say, 'Okay I've done it. Now I can relax.' No, the truth is you have to create something new all the time.

"You can't build an empire by not loving what you're doing, and you have to live it and breathe it every day. It's a long, hard, uphill climb and keep in mind, getting to the top is very challenging, but staying there is even tougher. Look at Microsoft, look at Apple. Even they have competition.

"It can also be very stressful…but not if you learn how to enjoy it. Fortunately, I love what I do. What keeps me going is the joy I get from knowing that I'm going to leave something behind, that I have contributed something to the world that didn't exist before I was here. And even though it may be true that nothing lives forever, we know that ORLY is going strong and that we still have a long journey ahead of us. I can't tell you how glad I am to be making that trip with all of you."

The rest of the evening is a blur of "thank yous" and embraces, all tinged with the sadness of good-byes. And while we know that we'll see many of these people again, there are others we may not. But for this one night we have joyously shared these moments with each other in a special way that will last for the rest of our lives.

Jeff Pink and Elsbeth Schutz, Celebrity
Manicurist/ORLY's Ambassador and Educator, at one
of our international distributor's showroom, 1998.

Slovakia and Czech Republic distributors, Milan and Beata Slimak.

Greek distributors Dora Kyprioti and Liarakos Nikos with Jeff Pink.

Ukraine distributor Natalia Tereschenko.

UK distributors Lorraine Jackson and Jon Hardwick.

Cypress distributor Paris Menelaou.

ORLY distributors eagerly watching a presentation
at the conference.

Lithuanian distributor Domas Lygnugaris.

Japanese distributor Etsuzo Tomita.

Italian distributor's legendary sales manager,
Gilberto Pietrantoni, of Ladybird.

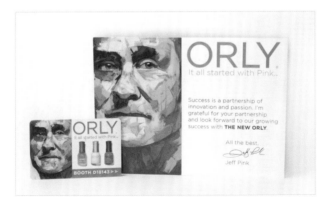

Welcome note made by Jeff to conference participants
along with a custom hotel room key.

Cindy Cebulak representing ORLY at an
international conference, 2017.

International Distributors visiting ORLY's headquarters.

17

HOW TO RUN A COMPANY

The "complete makeover" has changed the face of ORLY. We decide to run the "IT ALL STARTED WITH PINK" campaign for two years. I'm happy to say that Carina was right about the market research. As a result of her good advice, the company is completely re-energized.

The Françoise Nielly painting featured in our advertising was hip, colorful, creative, and futuristic. I received a lot of attention from it. It's not that the average person on the street recognized me from the ads. After all, the painting was an abstract and only people who knew me could see that it was my face portrayed in the myriad of colored blocks. But there was definitely a change in the way that I was viewed by my peers—as if the painting had elevated me to a higher status. In addition, there was a distinct change in the public perception of ORLY. Once again, we attained a position of relevance as an exciting and forward-thinking company. The marketing division and the Françoise Nielly painting had done an excellent job.

As a result of the "IT ALL STARTED WITH PINK" ad campaign, I'm being invited to speak all over the world. I take off on a tour to Australia, England, Russia, the United Arab Emirates (Dubai to be precise), and Italy with my public relations director,

John Galea. Everywhere we go, I'm asked to do more interviews than originally planned for television, fashion magazines, and radio. The journalists all want to know about the company and about me, but mostly they want to know about the Original French Manicure.

As much as I resisted having my image featured in our advertising campaign, I see now how beneficial it has been for ORLY. The company is getting a lot more recognition and we can see the results in our international sales growth.

As I travel around the world, I make it a point to meet with many of the people I first encountered back in the early 1990s when I started to develop the international market. It's great to see so many of them still working with ORLY. Almost twenty-five years have passed and now they look at me not just as someone trying to do business with them, but also as a senior statesman, an authority on the nail business.

Everywhere we go, I'm introduced as the man who created The French Manicure. I'm always quick to say that ORLY is known for many great innovations, but by now I know that what people want to hear is a quick headline, something they can instantly relate to.

So I've stopped resisting and I go with the flow. I understand that if you're lucky enough to have done something that brought you worldwide recognition, then that's what you'll always be known for. So, I accept the role of successful businessman, entrepreneur, and creator of The French Manicure.

I quickly learn that in this new role, people are constantly asking me for advice. It's very flattering and confirms my own suspicion that I actually do know something. But giving advice can be tricky.

You never want to discourage someone who has a real passion to do something new, but you also don't want to encourage someone to do something that you can see they're not ready for. So when people call me for advice, I give as much as I can and I don't discourage them. I just tell them what to expect so they can be ready for it.

For example, a friend of mine has a daughter who wants to go into the cosmetic business, and he calls me on the phone and says, "Jeff, my daughter has a good idea for a skin care product, and she wants me to help her develop it. Before I invest in her idea, I thought maybe you could give me some advice." I say, "Bring your daughter to a meeting and we'll talk about it."

A few days later, they arrive at my office and I can see right away the young girl is bright-eyed, intelligent, and very enthusiastic. She says, "Thank you for seeing us, Mr. Pink. This product is so important to me and I really appreciate you taking the time to talk with us."

My assistant, Shaina, offers them water and espresso. No, they don't want anything to drink; they don't want to take up too much of my time. I appreciate that because often when people come for advice, they want to make it a social event—something I have no patience for. So I sit down with them and try to explain what's involved in building a company and creating a new brand.

"If you believe in your product so much that you're willing to give everything you have to make it happen, then you can do it. But keep in mind that it's not a question of just the money; it's a question of having the right people who are going to be there to help you do it. The big challenge is to find the right people...and that's not easy."

The girl looks at me with surprise. This was obviously not the answer she was expecting. "So maybe it would be better for me to sell my idea to a big company?"

I shake my head, "Listen, when you sell an idea to another company, what you give up is the excitement of fulfilling your dream and the feeling of accomplishment...and you don't get that much for selling it. But when you build a brand and it becomes successful and then you sell it to a big company, that's when you get a lot for it. So if you want to bring out a new product, then go for it. Identify companies that can sell you the materials for the product, for the packaging, for whatever you'll need. The most important thing I can tell you is this: you, as one person, cannot do everything."

I continue, "You have to know what it is that you can do best for this product, because you can be a good salesperson, or maybe a good marketer, or maybe you are just good at making the product. But to be successful, my advice is to do the things that you can do best and hire other people that can do the things you can't do yourself."

The girl looks at her father and takes a deep breath. I can see that some of the wind has gone out of her sails so I ask her, "What do you like to do best?" She says, "I like to come up with ideas and create the products, but to be honest, I don't know anything about marketing or sales."

I say, "That's good that you know that. So why don't you hire a salesperson or hire someone who can produce the product? Just don't try to do everything. You'll have your hands full running around trying to figure out 'Where can I buy this raw material?' 'Who can make the product?' 'How do I package the product?' It's a big process. What you need to do is go home and decide what you want to do. If you're ready, then go for it. If not, take some time to think about it."

A few days later, my friend calls me and says, "I want to thank you, Jeff. My daughter came to me and said she didn't realize that it's not that easy and that it requires so many things that she doesn't know anything about. She's decided not to do it right now, but to wait until she is ready. You probably saved me a lot of money, Jeff."

I tell him, "She's a smart girl and when she's ready, give her your support. That's what parents are for."

It always feels good when someone accepts my advice and it turns out well. One of the benefits for me is that when I'm telling people "how I did it," sometimes I realize that certain things I've learned along the way have stayed in my head and become pearls of wisdom.

That happened recently when I was asked, "If you were to retire who would you choose to run the company?" My immediate response was, "I would probably pick someone from marketing or finance, but not from sales." It has been my experience that marketing and finance people are looking at the long-term picture of the company, whereas salespeople are driven by short-term quotas.

My answer to the question was a knee-jerk reaction and I really had to think long and hard about it afterwards. Why was I so averse to appointing anyone from sales to run ORLY? It's certainly not that I don't respect the salespeople because, in truth, they have contributed greatly to the company's success.

My sales division is the backbone of ORLY, and to build a great sales team takes years. So why, I ask myself, did I have this instantaneous reaction?

As I think back, it must be related to the first experience I had with salespeople when I was going to school in Michigan and I wanted to buy a car. In those days, you would open the newspaper and see the car you wanted, which at that time cost about $2,500. And then you would see another ad offering the same, brand-new car for $999.

You're so happy to find it; you go to the dealer to buy it and he says, "Sit down, Mr. Pink. I guess you want the car we have for $999?" I say "Yes." He replies, "Mr. Pink, would you like to have tires on the car? Would you like to have seats in the car? A steering wheel?" It ends up costing $2,500. What they do is "bring you in." It's a very successful trick they play on you, but it left me with a bad impression regarding car salespeople.

Fortunately, nowadays they can't do that because every car ad has to be tied to a VIN number.

I realized too late that I had made a mistake with at least two people who were all great at selling, but in their eager pursuit of sales, they lost sight of the bigger picture and what would benefit the company as a whole, instead of just the sales department and sales results.

The best CEO you can get needs to have experience in many things: marketing, operations, finance, and sales...a little bit of everything. That's why entrepreneurs like me become successful— because they have had to do every job imaginable and they know about every aspect of running a company.

At the same time, it doesn't mean that one person has all the answers and a good CEO needs to know that too. As I always say, I like to work with people who are smarter than me and I like to hear their ideas and opinions. Even if I don't agree with them, I always listen to what they have to say. Sometimes their input makes my ideas better. But if I'm completely confident that my idea is best, I say, "Listen, guys, thank you for your ideas, but I want to do it differently."

I'm sure that at the meeting where we came up with the teaser ads for the Gripper Cap, there were people in the room who came up with different ideas, but that was one occasion where I knew exactly what I wanted to do. It was the same when I came up with the cow idea for launching the Calcium Shield nail strengthener at the convention in Las Vegas. Not everyone agreed with me, but that's what I wanted and it was right.

I'm more open to listening to other people when I don't have much experience in something or if I've never done it before. For instance, in 2011, our competitors introduced a new kind of nail product that was very successful called Soak-Off Gels, which replaced the old-style gels that were very durable but had a big problem. When it was time to remove the old-style gels, they had to be removed with an abrasive file or electric burr. The new soak-off gels could be removed without using a file, but it took up to twenty minutes to remove the gels from the nails by soaking them in a solvent. I didn't think that customers would have the patience to sit there for that long and so I was really against the idea altogether. My VP of Marketing, Carina, twisted my arm and convinced me that we should introduce a line of soak-off gel color because this was the new trend that we shouldn't miss out on. She was totally right. I thank myself for listening to her. We developed our own formula which improved on the existing soak-off gel product. Our product required only ten minutes to remove, making it much more convenient for the customer. With a new product that we developed years later, we reduced the removal to five minutes. The marketing department rolled up their sleeves and worked diligently 24/7, and in 120 days, we had a full line of ORLY GelFX. This product was an instant success: easy, convenient, super-glossy, durable, and an improvement over our competition. Lesson learned: take a product the customer already likes and improve upon it.

In 2012 we developed a new portable Smart LED lamp, which looked like a smartphone and had two primary purposes: one was practicality, the other was for marketing ORLY's new GelFX products. The lamp had multiple features such as its compact size, and its ability to set and cure ORLY's soak-off gel colors. It was rechargeable in any USB port and convenient for traveling. From a marketing standpoint, we offered the lamp as a giveaway to salons when they ordered a certain amount of ORLY products. It became—as with many other ORLY inventions—an instant hit.

I'm always excited when someone thinks outside the box and comes up with a creative idea that I've never thought of. That happened in the early '90s when one of the people in the marketing department came up with an ingenious idea to promote color. He took a picture of penguins and painted them in beautiful ORLY colors. At the bottom of the picture was the slogan, "We've got the world seeing ORLY," part of the Life Is Color campaign.

When readers opened the magazine and saw penguins in color, that got their attention. "What the hell are colorful penguins doing in a beauty magazine?" Immediately, I loved what he came up with.

Fortunately, I know right away what I like and what I don't like, and I like the colorful penguins a lot! It was a very successful campaign. This year, to my amazement, my distributor in Poland put that image of the penguins on Facebook…almost twenty years later and it still holds up.

One thing I've learned for sure is that in every business there's a lot of success and failure; there's no perfect picture. Because we're all human beings who strive to do good, the negative things that happen stay in our minds more than the positive. I learned that lesson early on in the M.A.P seminar. There are certain events in business that will always be painful for me, like having to part ways with Veronica Reyes, who helped me through the most difficult time that ORLY ever faced.

I still have very powerful feelings about severing that relationship after sixteen years. I've continuously tried to make it up to her, especially a few years after she left ORLY and her son had an incident that put him into a coma, just like my son. I knew how much support a parent needs at that time and I reached out again to help her.

I know she was appreciative and recently we had this text message exchange.

Hi Jeff, just wanted to greet you with a very HAPPY BIRTHDAY (missed it by a day)!!! Hope you had a great celebration! Take very good care! You & ORLY hold a very special place in my heart. You had helped me during my difficult times. Someday, I hope to be able to repay you! Take very good care! Veronica

Hey Veronica, I thank u much for reminding me of my birthday, I've been so busy I almost forgot about it...I'm blessed to have a cheerful friend like u and it means the world to me. Let's plan to meet in April as I'm going to be very busy in March. Big Hug and a Kiss, Jeff

Jeff, After the experience that I went through with my son, my outlook & priorities in life have changed dramatically. I am taking more time to enjoy little things & be thankful for the little that we have. Take very good care, my friend.

Relax & just take some time off. See you later...Veronica

I owe great thanks to Veronica...for many things...but mostly for the fact that our friendship has continued despite her departure from ORLY. Reflecting back, maybe I did more good than bad. Maybe that's why I survived and why ORLY is doing so well. It's something I think about...a lot.

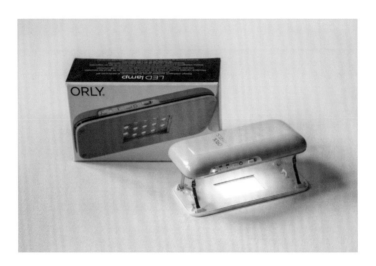

In 2012, ORLY introduced the Smart LED Lamp—the most compact and portable gel curing device on the market.

ORLY's new basecoat that made gel removal much easier.

ORLY's GelFX, pioneering in bold gel colors.

18

NEW COLOR COLLECTIONS

It's the "WOW" factor. You know it when you see it. It grabs your eye. It stops you in your tracks. It's intriguing and makes you want to know more. And finally, it makes you want to buy it.

That's the challenge we face several times a year. Up to six new colors every season, each new collection a completely original concept based on hundreds of hours of research and development, of writing and designing. All for one purpose: to excite our customers and capture our share of the ever-changing market. It's a highly-codified system, which has been honed and refined by marketing experts for the past thirty years.

As we sit down to start the process for the coming season and the holidays, I think back on what a long way we've come since we brought out the first ORLY color collection, when my wife, Orly, would come up with shades based on her own strong fashion instincts. That was in 1979, long before the nail industry had any sophisticated guidelines for developing a product that was seasonal and fashion-conscious.

That first collection came about in an almost random way. I was in the lab staring at a dozen bottles of polish that were lined up before me. I was searching for a new and interesting packaging idea.

I thought that maybe if I could come up with some kind of *thematic* concept instead of selling one new color at a time, we might be able to sell a collection of four, five, or six new colors all at once. In that era, all the nail colors were mostly various shades of red, mauve, maroon, and even brown.

As I started moving the bottles around, separating them into small groups ranging from the brightest red to the deepest maroon, it struck me that they looked like a miniature wine collection. I liked that idea, so I pulled six of my favorite proposed colors and put them together in what we called "The Winery Collection." Then, to add to the glamour, I gave each one a name that related to a Hollywood film star, like "Monroe Red" and "Crawford Wine."

I was kind of making it up on the spot, but even though I didn't know exactly what I was doing, it was a big success and ORLY became the first company in the nail industry to introduce a "themed collection." The "Winery" idea captured the imagination. I just started out by wanting to make an eye-catching package and as usual, I went with my gut feeling.

I had no idea that I was initiating a concept that would eventually become a strategic part of our marketing plans. Today, the process is far less organic and far more precise.

The way the nail industry operates today is on fashion predictions that look two years into the future. These are not merely informed guesses about what the coming trends will be, or casual suppositions on what people might like. They are carefully calculated decisions made by the mavens of the fashion industry.

The way it works is that every year, the fashion designers, along with the big fabric manufacturers and other power brokers of the fashion world, sit down together and decide what colors they'll be featuring two years in advance.

Once they've made their decisions, the fabric manufacturers create their new fabrics to accommodate the principal chosen colors; then various "trend agencies" create reports on the use of those colors in textiles. ORLY works with several of these agencies—including Peclers—in France, who forecast the trends for the coming year through a highly sophisticated process that starts on a socio-cultural level by connecting the dots between art, music, movies, literature and politics. From there, based on their findings, they can forecast consumers' needs and desires, including what kind of products or colors they will be receptive to in the coming season.

Based on these findings, fashion designers incorporate the new seasonal colors in their collections and then the cosmetic companies come up with their lip, eye or nail colors to work with what will be shown on the fashion runways.

All designs for future collections are created around the color palette that has been decided for the season, which is why we have so much color coordination every season in the fashion world.

Within that newly decided color palette, each company comes up with their own interpretations. Our blue may have a little more green than our competitors', or our pink may lean a little more towards orange. In that way, we each differentiate ourselves according to what we think our customers will respond to.

This is where ORLY gets down to the precision work of exploring the sociological trends, the color trends, and our own personal insights about the competitive environment. To help guide us in that phase we turn to WGSN, a company that specializes in socio-cultural and lifestyle trends. Their reports are utilized by our marketing division to come up with ideas and input to present to me. I give them feedback based on my years of experience and my gut feeling (yes, I still trust that!) and sometimes I'm very happy with what they show me, but sometimes I ask them for more. Even with all this highly scientific research, we still consider adding a color strictly on impulse from time to time.

Based on my feedback, product development goes to our color lab and sits down with the chemists, and together they come up with different color samples. Once those samples have been approved, we have a meeting and select the colors we want to test. That's when we start our initial consumer concept testing.

One of the best parts of the ORLY headquarters is that we have our own in-house salon/spa where we offer free manicures to women in the neighborhood. They try out the new products and give us their feedback.

Based on what we learn, the marketing and sales teams pull together their ideas for the new color theme. Around each new idea they create stories, mood boards, advertising copies, and present us with a wide range of creative input to feed the next steps in the development process.

This intense level of refinement goes on continuously with ideas bouncing back and forth among the different departments until they are ready to be presented to me for my approval. When we make that all-important final decision to move forward with a new collection, it's the result of the creativity of a brilliant team of specialists all working together. I have learned to trust them, so my involvement in selecting colors is much less than it once was.

Every year we develop between twenty-four and thirty new shades: six new colors for each season or special occasion, and in winter we do an additional Holiday Collection, which can be either new colors or colors that we've already developed and think will work well for the holidays. I have the deciding thumbs up or the thumbs down, but usually, by the time I am presented with the final choices, I like what I see.

It's a very sophisticated process and the highly successful results can be seen from some of our past collections. In the early 2000s our marketing division came up with a great idea...to create a "WEDDING COLLECTION." We've known for a long time how many women choose The French Manicure for their weddings, so it made a lot of sense to give them some options of having different color tips—pink, beige, and rose—to coordinate with the colors of their flowers, accessories, or bridesmaid dresses. I wholeheartedly approved the idea and Marketing came up with a unique display for salons and drug stores to present this innovative idea, which was exclusive to ORLY. Brides loved it and it became extremely popular. Several years later, in 2006, I came up with a completely opposite idea... "THE DIVORCÉE COLLECTION." Why not? People get married, people get divorced. This one we had some fun with...the colors had names like "Take Him To The Cleaners" and "One Night Stand." Magazines took notice and gave us a lot of publicity, some of it unwanted. A handful of religious organizations expressed a concern that we were promoting divorce. My attitude was "The only thing we're promoting is our product, and divorce is just a reflection of real life." There are always going to be critics...all you can do is move on.

One of our biggest winners came in 2013 when we created "SECRET SOCIETY," a holiday color collection that exceeded all of our expectations. Based on what were the predominant cultural trends that year, we developed a theme focusing on exclusive, speakeasy bars and clubs with private passwords that conjured extravagant gatherings in places of elaborate grandeur. The copy featured provocatively descriptive phrases such as "Intoxicating, opulent, an aristocratic palette of color cloaked in a culture of excess."

The colors were described as "edgy jewel tones and majestic metallics denoting luxury and wealth," with color names like, "Macabre Masquerade," "Risqué Encounter" and "Masked Ceremony." It was all about decadence and mystery. The display art featured seductive women wearing masks or veils and the polishes were filled with sparkling micas and glittering metallic pigments.

To support the collection, we created promotions and gift-with-purchases relating to the theme: lock and key necklaces, ornate bangles and lace gloves. "SECRET SOCIETY" was a resounding success.

Then in the summer of 2014, we surpassed ourselves with our best-selling collection to-date: "BAKED." The inspiration for that collection was based on saturated tropical tones with baked pigments. "A palette of primary colors, rainbow tones, neons, and brights." They were fluorescent, effervescent, dense, saturated, and energetic. The images associated with the collection were of tropical birds and lush jungle vegetation. The adjectives were "glowing, exciting, wild, festive, and vivacious."

There was something extra special about this "BAKED" collection. The bright neon shades have always been a favorite of ORLY customers. But this time we wanted to take the collection a step further. There was a trend in cosmetics towards "baked" products such as eye shadows and bronzers and we decided to apply that same technology to our formula by infusing our colors with baked pigments and finely ground specialty micas with the added benefit of vitamins and minerals. What our chemists delivered was an ultra-smooth polish with deeply rich colors and a superior shine.

The palette was an explosion of in-your-face color—from fuchsia to lime, neon orange and purple crème with names like "Tropical Hot," "Ablaze," and "Lush." Sales for "BAKED" went through the roof. The colors were so popular that many of them are now included in our permanent color assortment. Not every collection is a home run, but with "BAKED" we hit it out of the park.

In addition to our ongoing development of the seasonal collections, ORLY also creates private collections for companies that want to promote their business activities with merchandising. These collections are increasingly popular in the promotion of films like the ones we did for Warner Brothers and Disney which they sell in their theme parks, at Disney stores, and exclusively at Walgreens.

Sometimes you just get lucky and certain marketing ideas take on a life of their own. We never saw it coming, but that's exactly what happened in 2016 when, as part of the "MADE IN L.A." campaign, we came up with a new color collection we called "LA LA LAND." It was our tribute to the beauty and style of Los Angeles. Little did we know that a movie by that very same title was going to win six Academy Awards that year. Was it coincidence, good timing, or just plain good luck? Who knows? Whatever it was, it gave the collection an exciting boost and brought us a lot of attention.

You can see how far we've come since that first Winery Collection, and when I look back, I can't help but think about how different things were before the advancements in technology and marketing. It's like the remote for your television set—once it was nothing more than an on and off switch, but that was a time when life was simpler and straightforward. Today, if you want to stay in the game, you have to embrace the change or fall by the wayside. We've chosen to embrace the change…big time.

ORLY obtained the licensing rights to use this image of Marilyn Monroe promoting the "Monroe's Red" Color Collection.

SUMMER '95 BBSI

A Marilyn Monroe look-alike to attract ORLY distributors, introducing "Monroe's Red" Color Collection in Las Vegas at the BBSI Show, Summer of 1995.

The first ORLY color collection, The Winery. Each color was named after a movie star, 1980.

We've got the world seeing Orly.

Life Is Color, a great ad campaign using penguins.

19

MADE IN L.A.

It's 2013 and I'm at a dinner party at the home of a friend to celebrate the guest of honor, Eric Garcetti, who was just elected Mayor of Los Angeles. Eric is a good-looking young man, very well spoken, charming and the son of Gil Garcetti, the former District Attorney of Los Angeles. Eric is looking for support from the business sector and I like what he has to say. I tell him about ORLY and how, since I moved to Los Angeles from Israel in 1974, I've had a great love for this city. I go on to say that while other companies are leaving L.A. to take advantage of cheap labor and more business-friendly tax structures, we've chosen to stay here because I've always felt that our roots are here and that ORLY has always been associated with the L.A. lifestyle. "In fact," I say, "we're thinking of doing a new campaign based on the slogan 'MADE IN L.A.'" Garcetti gets very excited about that idea and says, "Jeff, if you ever need my help, call me. I'd like to support the 'MADE IN L.A.' campaign."

I file that in the back of my mind for future use. I'm very encouraged by Garcetti's success and I think it's going to mean good things for doing business in L.A. So, it's particularly painful for me when bureaucrats at L.A.'s Building and Safety Department make some extraordinary demands on ORLY.

It all starts when I decide to expand the production area in my headquarters in Van Nuys and add a new and modern cafeteria for my employees where they can have lunch, chat, and relax with their co-workers. We file an application for a building permit only to learn that the city has so many requirements that I have to hire a consultant to figure out what's going on.

Here I am, trying to do something nice for ORLY's 200 employees and instead of the city helping me, they're giving me a hard time. Like they say, "No good deed shall go unpunished."

What I learn from the consultant is that since the time we built our new headquarters in 2004, building codes have changed. Usually, when a building has been around for a while, only the new construction and remodeling must meet current code and the rest of the building is mostly left alone; the term used is "grandfathered in." Sometimes, however, the City Building and Safety Department wants to flex their muscles—and perhaps make extra money—by forcing you to upgrade everything to the new codes. We receive a list of building codes that must be addressed in order to qualify for building permits. It's as if we've opened Pandora's Box.

In the City's master plan, the street in front of ORLY is scheduled to be widened in twenty years. The City is demanding that I immediately move the fence and the front gate back two feet from where it is now to accommodate their future expansion plan.

This is not a simple matter. It's going to cost me thousands of dollars and it may reduce the number of parking spaces, which I really can't afford to lose. When I mention this to my consultant, he informs me, "If you make any change to the parking lot, there's another new rule that requires every two parking spots to have a tree and special watering system."

So now it's going to cost me over $200,000. This is getting more ridiculous by the minute. I don't understand why they are giving me such a hard time about something that's going to happen twenty years from now. "I'm willing to give a commitment letter saying that in twenty years, if I'm still the owner of the building, I'll meet their requirements." My consultant tells me that he can't assure me that this is going to work, and unfortunately, he comes back a few days later and tells me that the city has rejected my offer. Instead, he tells me, "Maybe you can leave the gate as it is for now, but you'll have to give the land to the city now."

I ask, "What's the consequence of doing that?" (Because I know there are always consequences.)

He responds, "You'll have to remove all the spikes from the gate. The City of Los Angeles doesn't allow spikes on their property because it may hurt some thieves when they jump over."

Incredulous, I say, "That's the purpose of it?!" He is not amused; he doesn't see the irony and there's no benefit in arguing with him. This is going to require an end run.

Then I think, "There's an L.A. Councilwoman in the Van Nuys district, Nury Martinez. Why don't I invite her over to visit ORLY. Maybe she can help us." She agrees, and when she arrives at the factory she's completely surprised. She says, "I've been the Councilwoman of this district for a long time and I never knew we had such a beautiful company here. Is there anything I can do to help you?"

Those are just the words I wanted to hear. Of course, I say, "Yes." Then, I tell her everything. I also make it very clear that I don't want to do anything illegal. She assures me that everything will be done properly, and she assigns one of her assistants to my case. A special ruling from the city is handed down which allows me to acquire the necessary building permits to move ahead with my renovation and expansion plans. It's a big relief. I can now focus my attention on our day-to-day business and kicking our "MADE IN L.A." campaign into high gear.

There are several reasons behind the "MADE IN L.A." campaign. First, is to let our customers know that ORLY's vegan and cruelty-free products are not cheaply made overseas, and second, is to communicate to our customers that ORLY's roots are deeply imbedded into the city of Los Angeles.

L.A. is truly an amazing place. People come here from all over the world to grab a piece of the spotlight. The lure of L.A. is impossible to ignore because in L.A. the entire city is an art scene.

New York may have fashion, but L.A. has style. And as everyone in the fashion business knows, "Fashion is seasonal; style is forever." ORLY came here over forty years ago and we became a part of L.A. and then L.A. became a part of us. That's the idea I want to get across in the "MADE IN L.A." campaign.

In order to roll out the campaign, I meet with my marketing and creative staff to discuss using teaser ads, which we had done when we introduced the ORLY Gripper Cap to the marketplace. This time I come up with a proposal about showing objects and inventions that were made in L.A.

The first teaser ad is a photograph of a fortune cookie with the tag line, "Where was it invented?" Everybody will say "China, right?" "Wrong...In L.A. 1931." Next, we show "The Apple Martini," also invented in L.A. Then a skateboard followed by a few other locally created objects, and finally The French Manicure, which everybody thinks was invented in France. "Wrong again ...MADE IN L.A."

We launch the campaign in *NAILPRO* and *NAILS*, national trade magazines. Then, after the intriguing questions have been running long enough to pique everyone's interest, we do the reveal of our latest product, EPIX Flexible Color.

I'm in my office going over sales figures, which are very gratifying, when my executive assistant, Shaina, buzzes me on the phone. There's a call from the mayor's office. I pick up the phone. "Hi, Jeff, it's Eric."

"Mr. Mayor, to what do I owe the pleasure?"

As it turns out, Nury Martinez, the councilwoman who helped me out with my permit problems, told the mayor how impressed she was with our facility. He's already aware of the "MADE IN L.A." campaign and he wants to come visit. This is fantastic! We're all very excited.

Shaina schedules a day and Mayor Garcetti's staff give us very specific instructions. "The mayor is going to visit you between noon and 12:20 p.m. and he's on a very tight schedule." We assure them that we understand but also that we would be happy to have him stay for as long as he can.

The day arrives and ORLY is decked out in its finest. Everything is spotless; there are fresh flowers on all the desks and everyone has dressed up for the occasion. The mayor's aides arrive at 11:45 a.m. and very officiously inform me that Mayor Garcetti will be arriving in a few minutes and whatever I plan to show him, I should do it as fast as possible because he has many other appointments on his schedule. I assure them that I'll stick to the schedule. Suddenly, everyone is peering out of their office doors and looking into the reception area. The glass doors open wide and there he is. He strides towards me with a big smile, nodding and saying hello to all the people in the hallway, then grasps my hand in something between a handshake and a hug. "What a beautiful place you've got here, Jeff."

Mayor Eric Garcetti is as warm and friendly as he was the night we first met during dinner at my friend's house. He looks around at the wonderful photographs on our walls and the colorful displays in our showroom and he pulls out his phone and asks, "Can I take some pictures?" Right away he posts them on Instagram. And that's how it goes for close to an hour as I give him a tour of our headquarters, explaining the function of each department and pointing out our automated production equipment, which I'm particularly proud of.

He's relaxed and comfortable and paying very little attention to his aides, who keep reminding him of the time. Before he leaves, I say, "I have something else I would like you to see." His people insist that he has to go but he says, "No." He wants to take a look at whatever I have to show him.

My oldest son, Ran, has become a professional recording artist and his music studio is attached to our headquarters. I take the mayor in to meet Ran, who's at the piano working on a composition, and the mayor says, "Can I play with you?" And he sits down at the piano. We're all having so much fun that when his aides insist that it's time to go, he says jokingly, "You go on without me. I'm having too good a time." The mayor's twenty-minute visit turns into an hour and half, and in that time, we cement our friendship.

Los Angeles Mayor Eric Garcetti visiting ORLY's headquarters along with Councilwoman Nury Martinez, meeting with Jeff Pink and ORLY staff.

"MADE IN L.A." teaser campaign, 2016.

"MADE IN L.A." teaser campaign, 2016.

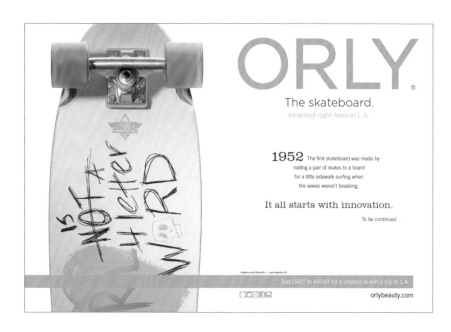

"MADE IN L.A." teaser campaign, 2016.

"MADE IN L.A." teaser campaign, 2016.

ORLY®

EPIX. Made in L.A.

2015 ORLY, the home of innovation, brings you the next big thing in the industry. A new generation of nail color, a brand new category... Flexible Color.

It all starts with innovation in L.A.

nailpro.com/freeinfo • use freeinfo #1   Text ORLY to 44144 for a chance to win a trip to L.A.

          orlybeauty.com

"MADE IN L.A." campaign final reveal, 2016.

ORLY introduces a brand-new hybrid color collection,
EPIX—2014, in the "MADE IN L.A." campaign.

20

MAKING THE CHANGES

You can never underestimate the effect world affairs has on business, even the nail business. Over forty years ago, as a result of the Vietnam War, the nail industry was changed forever. It happened in a most unlikely place, Hope Village, a Vietnamese refugee camp in Northern California.

American film star, Tippi Hedren, who is best known for her starring role in the Alfred Hitchcock film *The Birds,* is also a philanthropic humanitarian. She saw the plight of hundreds of Vietnamese women refugees who had ended up in Hope Village and who had no way to support themselves in the United States.

Hedren brought in a variety of instructors to teach the refugees new skills like sewing and typing. But what really fascinated the women were Tippi's beautifully manicured nails. They wanted to know how to do that. So Tippi flew in her personal manicurist to teach a group of refugee women the art of manicure. The women proved to be highly adept and perfectly suited to this new profession.

They loved the work and were soon teaching it to all the other women in the camp. That handful of women went on to radically transform the nail industry, which today is dominated by Vietnamese-Americans.

Not only were these women naturally gifted in the art of manicure, many of them were also good businesswomen. Within a few years, Vietnamese-owned nail salons sprang up everywhere with a new added feature: these salons were able to accommodate walk-in trade.

Rather than one manicurist in a hair salon who required a booking well in advance, these salons offered the flexibility of walk-in business that perfectly suited the lifestyle of working women, who could get a manicure on the spur of the moment. What was equally appealing to budget-conscious working women was that their prices were much lower because the nail salons had so many manicurists on staff. Suddenly, it seemed like the cost of a manicure dropped overnight from $30 to $15, and a combo manicure/pedicure could be had for less than $25.

It was a seismic shift in the nail industry that prompted many other changes, including a demand for more interesting colors, fashion decals, and outrageous nail designs.

The Vietnamese salon owners were more comfortable doing business with distributors who spoke their own language, so eventually ORLY started working with Vietnamese-American distributors. These salon owners were reliable customers and eager to learn about new products. All in all, it became a very satisfying business relationship for ORLY and for other nail care product companies.

All was going well until a manufacturer here in California made a gripper cap similar to ours, copying our design and infringing on our utility patent—that is, until they were informed by our attorney that they were in violation of the law.

The beauty of a patent is that it protects both the design and the utility. In our case, they were using both. We went to arbitration. The owner spoke halting English and the arbitrator explained very carefully, "Do you know that in the US there is a law known as Intellectual Property, which protects patents and trademarks? You have to obey this law. You can't copy Mr. Pink. You are taking his property."

The owner seemed truly embarrassed and said, "In the country I came from, we don't have this issue. We can copy from anybody." The arbitrator replied, "Well you live in the United States and must abide by our laws. Here, you can't do that." The owner apologized and agreed to pay a fine, promising never again to use anyone's patent illegally.

In that particular case, I think the owner truly did not know the law, but it happened to us a few other times when the perpetrator did know the law and was just trying to get away with it. It's usually the small companies that do that kind of thing because the big companies know they'll get sued.

The small companies think they have nothing to lose. But if you're the patent holder, you have to go after the perpetrator and defend yourself even if the law is on your side. The government won't do the work for you; they just issue you a patent to announce to the world that "Mr. Jeff Pink of ORLY owns a patent to manufacture and use a patented Gripper Cap, so please be aware of it." But some companies don't care. And once one of them does it, others will follow. Even though you own a patent, it's up to you to protect it. You have to be vigilant and have a good lawyer to represent you in court if it comes to that.

The government, in addition to creating laws which are intended to protect against product infringement, also has an effect on business through the establishment of environmental regulations that are aimed at protecting the public. One such regulation stimulated the development of the soak-off nail gel. Nail companies were required to remove certain ingredients from nail polish. The removal of these ingredients made manicures short-lived and the industry responded with a new kind of gel polish that had an even longer life than the original nail polish. That was a big plus, but there were also some minuses.

The new gel requires more steps in its application. It's a longer process and every time you apply a coat, you have to put it under an LED lamp. That's the blue UV light device that you put your hands in to quickly cure each coat. It works very well and it lasts up to two weeks. But the big problem with gel is that you can't remove it as easily as nail lacquer and some women may be sensitive to gel as it may damage the top layer of their nails.

Our product, EPIX Flexible Color, which we introduced in our "MADE IN L.A." campaign, is a "hybrid." It looks shiny like gel and removes nail polish. It's easy to apply, and there is no need for a base coat. The product only needs a topcoat, and it's not necessary to use an LED lamp because regular light cures it in eight minutes. Some customers are turning to this new technology in nail color as it becomes easier to use and more cost effective.

This is all part of the business; the constant assessing and correcting of problems and the changing demands of the marketplace. It's how innovation takes place. People are always looking for something new and improved. For example, I work as a consultant with a company that is developing a patented machine that you put your hand into and it paints your nails. It's amazing and I'm sure you'll be seeing it on the market before long.

And who would have ever thought that religion would have an effect on the nail business? Well, in certain countries it does. When I started to do business in Saudi Arabia, they were buying so much product that I was concerned that they were diverting and selling it to other countries, which we don't allow. Once, when I was in Dubai, I decided to go to Saudi Arabia to find out what the distributor is doing with so much nail polish. What I discover is that Muslim women are not allowed to wear nail polish on their fingers when they pray or perform any religious rituals. Before prayer, Muslim women must wash from their hands down to their elbows in a ritual called Wudu and consider anything standing between their skin and the water as a barrier and therefore a problem. That means a woman must remove her nail polish before she prays and then reapply it again later. No wonder our polish is in demand.

A similar concept is found in the Jewish faith and it is called mikvah. This is a ritual bath which a woman takes at particular times, especially right before the wedding ceremony. Women cannot have any adornments on their body in the mikvah, including nail polish.

21

HAPPY FORTIETH ANNIVERSARY

It's May of 2015, and as I pull into the parking lot at ORLY headquarters in Van Nuys, I can feel a sense of excitement vibrating in the air. As soon as I walk through the front door, I see that everyone is dressed up. Every face greets me with a big smile. We all know it's a very special occasion because this year we are celebrating the fortieth anniversary of the founding of ORLY.

For days, I've been trying to wrap my head around that fact. "How did forty years go by so fast?" I was a young man when I started, and now I have children as old as I was then. It is true what they say, "Life goes by in the blink of an eye." That's why it's important that we stop to observe these special occasions.

This year, as an added feature of our International Conference, we will be celebrating our anniversary. People will fly in from all over the world to spend a few days in Los Angeles. We'll do our best to make it an unforgettable experience. The conference guests are housed at the beautiful Santa Monica beach hotel, Le Merigot. On the first evening, we hold a welcome reception at the beachfront hotel, serving dinner with live music in the background that people can dance to throughout the evening. Because many of the guests had come from overseas, the evening ended early so everyone would be well-rested. The next morning, the conference started with presentations and education about our new products. On the second night of the conference, we gather for dinner at the famed Perch restaurant in downtown Los Angeles. Built on the historic 1923 Pershing Square Building, the Perch is a French inspired rooftop bistro with breathtaking views of downtown Los Angeles. It's going to be a night to remember! I invite Mayor Garcetti to join us for dinner. I know how busy he is, but I am delighted to receive a note from the mayor's chief of staff that the mayor will be there.

At every conference, awards are given out to our top international distributors. This year, the accolades will go to Ladybird in Italy for Excellence in Marketing, and to EVA Beauty in Greece for Excellence in Professional Development, with Honorable Mentions to companies in New Zealand, Lithuania, Russia, the UK, and Slovakia.

It was no surprise who the two top recipients were, as they have been honored before. The stories of how they became leading distributors are similar. Twenty-four years ago, in 1995, when I was spending most of my time overseas building our international business, I met two Italian sisters, Libera and Cinzia Ciccomascolo, at the Cosmoprof Bologna Beauty Show, which is the largest beauty show in the world. At the time, they were giving manicures in a temporary tent separate from the main, permanent pavilions. They approached me and said they would like to represent ORLY in Italy, and they were hoping to set up a company for importing products to sell to professional manicurists. Initially, I had my doubts that they were qualified to take on such an important assignment, but I didn't have a distributor in Italy at the time. After spending a few hours with them at the show, I realized that they were powerful women and that with further knowledge and education from us, they would be an excellent addition to our international network of distributors.

I trusted my instincts and it paid off for all of us. Over the years, they established a formal company, Ladybird, and won many awards from ORLY—more than any other distributor up until today. Our relationship with them grew rapidly and we became close friends—just like family. I call Cinzia and Libera "The Two Angels from Modena," a play on where their business is located.

The company recognized for Excellence in Marketing for 2015, EVA Beauty from Greece, became part of ORLY in a similar way. Liarakos Nikos and Dora Kyprioti approached me at Cosmoprof in 2001. Liarakos, a businessman, and Dora, a talented manicurist, were husband and wife. They said, "We are a couple and we would like to team up with you to represent ORLY in our country. Please give us a chance, and we will prove that you made the right decision." And they surely did. Whoever would have thought that a couple that built a distribution center for nail products in Greece—a small country—would win many awards, which they keep doing for many years.

When the big night arrives to present the awards, we're all gathered in the magical rooftop dining room at Perch at 7:00 p.m. Below us, the city sparkles like diamonds against a black velvet sky. Twinkling lights and lanterns decorate the rooftop and cast a warm glow on the fashionably attired guests. Great music wafts from the turntable of the DJ, who has been hired to play all the different kinds of music I love, from Tony Bennett, Paul Anka, to current hits that make you want to shake your butt and compel you to dance.

I look around at the smiling faces, which include my longtime close friend, Jack Sperling, Deborah Carver, the publisher of *NAILPRO* Magazine, and my children—Ran and his wife Shel (who also is the founder of "SPARITUAL," a part of the ORLY Group), my son Tal, and my daughter Shanee—and so many other people who have meant so much to me and to ORLY over the years. My heart is brimming with gratitude and joy.

We are just about ready for dinner when the mayor's chief of staff arrives. He is shown over to where I am standing and says, "I'm sorry, Mr. Pink, but Mayor Garcetti just flew back from Washington, D.C. and I don't think he's going to be able to make it here tonight." Naturally, I'm disappointed, but I accept his apology and invite him to join us as the representative of the mayor. He declines, but I can't help feeling that something is going on because why would the chief of staff show up just to tell me that the mayor isn't going to be there?

We all sit down to dinner. The waiters are pouring wine and passing baskets of bread when, across from the dinner table, I see the rooftop elevator doors open and two men step out. At first, I think it must be some late arrivals but as they come closer, I see it's the mayor's chief of staff and next to him is the mayor of Los Angeles, Eric Garcetti, smiling from ear to ear.

I can hear the ripple of excitement on the rooftop as the mayor enters and comes directly to my table. I stand up to tell him how honored I am that he is here. He shakes my hand, gives me a hug, and turns to all the guests, welcoming them to the City of Los Angeles and says, "And this is for you, Jeff." He hands me a beautifully engraved plaque, an official Proclamation from the City of Los Angeles inscribed to JEFF PINK and ORLY in commemoration of the "MADE IN L.A." campaign. This is beyond my wildest dreams. Not only has the mayor presented me with this wonderful gift, but he stays for the whole dinner and patiently has his picture taken with our distributors and my family. It's another night that none of us will ever forget.

I decide we're going to stick with the campaign, "MADE IN L.A." I believe it works for us, not just in L.A., but all over the world.

Photos from ORLY's International Conference held at Le Merigot Beach Hotel & Spa in Santa Monica, CA, May 3rd – 4th, 2015.

ORLY's welcome desk at the International Conference located at Le Merigot Beach Hotel & Spa, Los Angeles, 2015.

Cindy Cebulak, ORLY's fabulous tradeshow manager.

Photos from ORLY's International Conference held at Le Merigot Beach Hotel & Spa in Santa Monica, CA, May 3rd – 4th, 2015.

Celebrity manicurist, Elsbeth Schutz, at ORLY's International Conference in Los Angeles, 2015.

John Galea, ORLY's Director of Communications.

Libera and Cinzia Ciccomascolo of Ladybird, the "Two Angels of Modena."

Photos from ORLY's International Conference held at Le Merigot Beach Hotel & Spa in Santa Monica, CA, May 3rd – 4th, 2015.

Jeff Pink and Japanese distributor, Etsuzo Tomita.

Jeff and his son, Tal Pink.

Photos from ORLY's International Conference held at Le Merigot Beach Hotel & Spa in Santa Monica, CA, May 3rd – 4th, 2015.

Jeff Pink & Carina Breda, ORLY's VP of Marketing.

Bill Korn, ORLY's VP of Operations.

Photos from the 40ᵗʰ Anniversary party at the Perch in downtown L.A. with Eric Garcetti, and ORLY International Distributors May 4, 2015.

The Pink Family with L.A. Mayor.
(Left to right) Tal Pink, Jeff Pink, Eric Garcetti,
Ran and Shel Pink.

Jeff Pink and Mayor Eric Garcetti.

Tal Pink watches with a big smile as Jeff greets Jack Sperling with a hug upon his arrival to the party.

Photos from the 40th Anniversary party at the Perch in downtown L.A. with Eric Garcetti, and ORLY International Distributors May 4, 2015.

Jeff Pink with his daughter, Shanee Pink.

(Left to right) Jeff Pink, Carina Breda, Eric Garcetti, John Galea, and Catherine Baek.

Photos from the 40th Anniversary party at the Perch in downtown L.A. with Eric Garcetti, and ORLY International Distributors May 4, 2015.

Jeff Pink and Italian distributors.

UK distributor team. (Left to right) Jon Hardwick, Lorraine Jackson, and Thea Lacey.

Photos from the 40th Anniversary party at the Perch in downtown L.A. with Eric Garcetti, and ORLY International Distributors May 4, 2015.

(Left to right) Jack Sperling, Deborah Carver, and Jeff Pink.

Elyse Piwonka and Elissa Mark of ORLY's marketing team.

22

FRESH THINKING

It's a warm afternoon in late summer and I'm sitting in my conference room with three of the most intelligent, talented, good-looking, young people I know...my children Ran, Tal, and Shanee Pink. I may be slightly biased, but even an objective observer would have to admit that these are three very special people and I feel lucky to have them involved in the future of ORLY.

It was always my secret wish that at least one of my children would follow in my footsteps to carry on the ORLY brand, but it was never a demand I forced on them. Their mother, Orly, and I encouraged them to find their own paths and to follow their own dreams, and that's exactly what each of them did. From their mother, they inherited a talent and a love for music. I never played an instrument but ever since I was a teenager, I've been considered a walking encyclopedia of popular songs.

When they all decided to pursue careers in music after college, Orly and I were one hundred percent supportive. Ran formed a band with a partner, Herwig Maurer, who he met at the Berklee College of Music in Boston where they were both students. The band was named MLF, "Mankind Liberation Front." RCA Records believed in their future and invested a lot of money in them. They never took off with the kind of hit that would make them famous but they recorded and toured, performing on big stages throughout the country.

Tal, who went to the University of Pennsylvania but later graduated in International Law from Warwick University in the UK, came back to the States with a law degree but ultimately decided to join Ran in the pursuit of making music. Their new band, Remote, was Beatle-esque and enjoyed success playing music in feature films and television shows. This led to Ran creating his own recording facility called "Fonogenic Studios." Tal moved his own business dealings into Fonogenic.

Their younger sister, Shanee's, music career started when she formed a successful duet with Mark Noseworthy, known as "Pink and Noseworthy." Their music received great reviews, such as the one in *Keyboard Magazine* that said: "The music of Pink and Noseworthy is rooted in classic '60s and '70s pop, yet it exists in a universe all its own, a seductive and lush melodic world that radiates a timeless presence, wrapped in a sparkling veneer of quality and fidelity."

The band lasted quite a while until Shanee decided to perform as a soloist, which she did for about ten years and which she still does from time to time, especially for charity events. Again, I may be biased but I thought their music was as good as anything I heard on the radio. The common thread of Ran, Tal, and Shanee's musical careers is that they all write and perform their own original music and lyrics.

Their mother, Orly, and I are among their biggest fans and followed their careers with great pride. I never missed a concert unless I was out of the country. I loved hearing them make beautiful music together.

At some point, their interests began moving beyond the music world. Ran had always been interested in the world of mentalism and magic as a kid, and he started to create and sell his own original techniques, garnering attention and fans from well-known performers in the magic world. Tal formed a tech startup, Dopetracks, which was a platform for hip hop music and an online community for musicians to connect. Shanee, in addition to her own musical pursuits, became a producer, promoter, and designer of musical events. Wherever their talents took them, we were happy to see them follow their individual paths—as long as they remained productive, happy individuals.

Then, much to my surprise, in the past three years, each of my children came to a decision on their own that it was time for them to become part of ORLY. Tal had just left a tech startup where he served as Director of Products and was the first to join the company as Digital Director. I asked him what made him decide to become part of the family business. He said, "Dad, I've done my own entrepreneurial projects. I realize how much work goes into doing your own thing. I looked at the amazing company that you've put together and I see tremendous potential to keep it growing. It was the perfect hybrid of working for a company that I already have a stake in and being able to join an established team of really talented people."

Ran is the new Content Creator and expressed his reasons for joining the company this way, "I always admired your ability to go after your dreams and roll up your sleeves to make them happen, Dad. But I had some hesitations about all of us working together. All I could imagine were the kinds of heated arguments and passionate discussions we had when we were younger and about how things would get very emotional. Now we're more mature and I think the timing worked out so we all can handle each other in a room."

Shanee came to work at ORLY in 2015 as Creative Director with her own personal vision, "This is a huge operation that needs to keep running. ORLY provides jobs for many employees and I had a realization that one day the future of this company will be our responsibility. I'd rather get involved now with the benefit of Dad's guidance."

I'm honored that my children want to join ORLY and I'm happy that we're finally working together. Each of them has earned their stripes at the company, learning from the bottom up. As Tal says, "We've always had our fingers and toes in the business, starting out with summer jobs when we were teenagers from working in the warehouse to taking orders." Now all three are helping bring a new look and style to ORLY.

These days, with technology moving so fast, I know that the best way to stay ahead of the game is to have input from young people who not only recognize the coming trends, but are also the same people shaping them.

Today Ran, Tal, and Shanee are meeting with me to discuss a number of company issues that each of them is involved with. We sit around the long mahogany and pewter table in our conference room and Shanee talks about the focus of our marketing outreach— specifically how we are defining the "ORLY woman." As we listen to her presentation and bounce ideas off one another, I can't help but feel a sense of pride in how much intelligence and creativity they each bring to the company.

It's a wonderful notion that a family can all work together happily, but it's not always a reality. In our family, each of us has a strong personality, and over the years we have had our differences. But working together was something that we all wanted and we knew that it would take some effort to make it work well. As Shanee once observed, "The same skills that it takes to work out a song with a band are the skills that it takes to get along with each other in business. We have to listen respectfully to each other's ideas. We have to disagree when we feel strongly and make a clear case for why we think differently about an idea and then, hopefully, it will lead to a new and better idea encompassing what everyone has brought to the process." As a family, what works for us is that we're all creative, but we're also very much aligned and can recognize a good idea no matter which of us comes up with it.

At our meeting today, Shanee—as the Creative Director—is elaborating on her idea that the ORLY woman is someone with style and elegance, who embodies the qualities that their mother, Orly, represents. Shanee has an interesting concept about branding the new ORLY collections with a focus on women who are successful in any discipline—cutting edge women who are self-reliant. We listen with great interest because as Shanee reminds us, she is our typical customer—a woman in her early thirties, stylish and fashion forward. Tal acknowledges the irony of growing up in a business where he is part of the one-half of society that historically didn't use the product. Ran adds that more men than ever are using nail polish. This leads to some lighthearted banter, some jokes and laughter, and eventually some concrete ideas about Shanee's proposal. There's real enthusiasm for her concept and some serious discussion about the financial aspects and the marketing feasibility of such a program.

Before we wrap up, Tal and Shanee lay out a concept that they have been working on for some time. Tal reminds us, "When we were kids, everyone used to ask us how the company came up with the names for our polishes."

Everyone nodded. "Well we've been thinking about a way to engage our customers more actively—something that has never been done before. The idea is called Color Labs—a store where customers can create and name their own custom polishes using an app and name their polish, too. It will be an experiential space of sorts, and if it works, we can replicate it. Right now, we are looking at a location near the Grove, which is one of the most successful outdoor malls in the city."

I said, "When you get further along, Tal, we need to sit down, go over the budget, and take a look at the design for the space. It reminds me of the wonderful boutique pharmacies that were all over Paris back in the '50s. An intimate space where women were catered to."[1]

I sit here listening to their creative ideas, their business savvy, and how they respect one another, and I know without a doubt that the future of ORLY will be safe in their hands. They understand that it's not just their financial future at stake; it's the future of the hundreds of employees who have been loyal supporters of our brand, and who depend on the success of the company. I know my children will be ready to pick up the reins when the time comes.

What I know for sure is that having my children with me running the company makes me feel that ORLY is a truly invested team and that there are so many people who are currently helping to continue the success of ORLY. I am not just one man opening a store in Tarzana but part of a great organization that will innovate and contribute to the beauty industry.

---

[1] In 2019 Color Labs finally opened to crowds lining outside the store. Customers can create custom nail polish using an app and then watch their shade brought to life by mixologists at the color bar. The space holds events such as master classes for nail art, color theory, ongoing artist in residence with well-known nail artists, and collaborative pop ups with other brands.

Shanee Pink in front of the ORLY Color Labs storefront,
Los Angeles, 2019.

The Next Generation.
(Left to right) Ran, Shanee, and Tal Pink with Jeff.

Jeff Pink and daughter in-law, Shel Pink, founder of
Sparitual, at the Croatia Conference, June 2017.

EPILOGUE

The beat goes on. Just when the ink dried on the last chapter, two new exciting events took place at ORLY which I am compelled to write about—the introduction of two new products and the special international recognition of ORLY from the beauty industry that came as a complete, yet gratifying surprise.

Forty-four years ago, in 1975, when I first started ORLY, I was interested in creating products that would allow a woman to grow her own nails naturally. I never wanted to provide any products for artificial nail extensions because the material that was used at that time and is still used today had a terrible smell and was bad for the nails. It was also a labor-intensive process that involved mixing powder and liquid, and the manicurists often wore breathing masks to protect themselves from the toxic fumes. Over the years, I never found any product for building sculptured and artificial nails that I was willing to put my company name on. But I did think about it...a lot. I knew the challenge was to create a product that worked easily, that didn't smell bad, and didn't damage the nails.

In 2015, we decided to go back to the drawing board and work extensively with several suppliers of raw materials to create my dream product of building a unique nail extension that would not damage the natural nail and would not have all the negative side effects of existing products. Once again, our inhouse spa, which we built for testing new and existing products, tested all the submissions but all were rejected.

Two years and countless attempts later, in a meeting with our vice president of marketing and our director of new product development, they gave me the bad news, "Jeff, I think we should just scrap the idea of nail extensions from the list of products in development. It's just not going to work. We are wasting our time." My immediate reaction was that I was not going to give up on the dream—at least not YET.

In the midst of discussing any and all potential solutions, something was burning in my brain about one of our products that had special ingredients that protected nails from breaking and splitting (a perennial problem). I shared this idea in detail with Dan Werner, our veteran chemist.

After several months of hard work in the laboratory and months of intense testing in our spa supervised by Colleen Foxworthy, a new product was born in record-breaking time, which we called Builder in a Bottle. To launch a groundbreaking product is hard enough, but to do it in less than six months is almost unthinkable. Formulas have to be proven, education protocols need to be developed, packaging must be designed, and components need to arrive in time to be manufactured into a finished product. Then, marketing has to launch a big campaign both digitally and in print. I had challenged the team to do the near impossible and they exceeded my expectations through hard work and ingenuity. It showed what real teamwork can accomplish. It was also the first major launch in which the whole Pink family worked together to make sure we executed on a high level. Finally, because this was a truly novel formulation, we made sure to apply for a patent during the development phase.

The uniqueness of the product is expressed in its name, Builder in a Bottle. It comes ready to apply in a single bottle, and there is no need to mix different ingredients. You just brush it on using nail forms of the desired length file, shape, and voilà—dream nail sculpting and extensions at your fingertips that are easy to apply!

Builder in a Bottle was introduced to the professional salon business in the United States in July 2018 at the Cosmoprof North America Show in Las Vegas. We made sure that the product would get the full attention of our professional distributors as a new innovation and game changer in building nail extensions. We had educators there to demonstrate the product and hand out special brochures explaining its features. Orders poured in and it was an instant success. In October 2018, we officially introduced the Builder in a Bottle to our international distributors at a special event held in Krakow, Poland. Krakow has special meaning to me because it is my father's birthplace. On the last day of the convention, our distributors called the innovation MAGIC.

The second great event happened in July 2018 when I got an e-mail from Raymond Meyboom, our distributor in France: "Jeff I want to let you know that ORLY has been nominated for the 2018 award for developing the BREATHABLE polish. That's all I can say for now, but I'll tell you more when it gets closer."

Naturally I want to hear everything. "Raymond, what kind of an award?" As it turns out, the French give out awards every year to companies that develop something new and innovative in the beauty industry and the judges have decided that ORLY'S one-step Breathable polish fits that description. The truly innovative aspect of the polish is that it's porous, and because air and moisture don't get trapped between the nail and the polish, it stays on much longer than regular polish. Obviously, the French are as enthusiastic about this product as we are and it's a big honor for an American company to be nominated for the award, the "Victoire de la Beauté."

The award ceremony is held in September 2018 in Paris during Fashion Week. When I learn that we have won, I decide to go to Paris to receive the award. I wouldn't miss it for anything.

The ceremony takes place at the famous Casino de Paris on the Rue de Clichy and is done in a tastefully lavish style as only the French can do. The Casino venue is filled with live music bands, colored lights, and beautiful people fashionably dressed. Friends and distributors from France, Belgium, and the Netherlands have all come to see me accept the award. When I am called to the stage, Raymond accompanies me as my interpreter because everyone else is speaking French. I know exactly what I'm going to say. I tell the audience, "I came all the way from Los Angeles for two reasons. The first reason is to accept the award for the BREATHABLE polish as the most innovative product in 2018, and the second reason is to thank the French people for allowing me to use the word 'French' in my biggest innovation ever, The French Manicure." The room went crazy; the people were laughing and cheering and clapping. It was such a wonderful feeling of coming full circle from the first time we showed The French Manicure in a Paris runway show so many years ago. Everything that has happened to me and ORLY has been as a result of that famous creation. It only seemed right to thank the French. *Merci beaucoup, mes amis. Vive la France!*

Jeff points to his newest invention,
Builder in a Bottle in 2018.

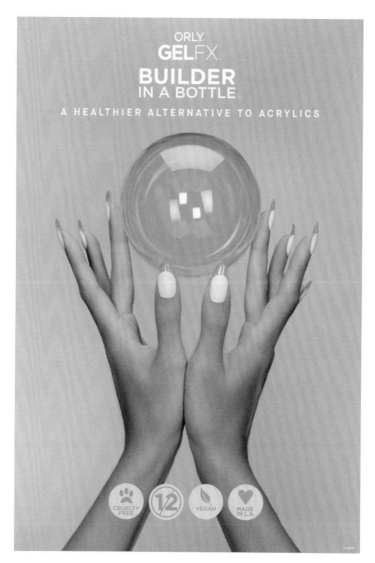

A great look for the Builder in a Bottle campaign.

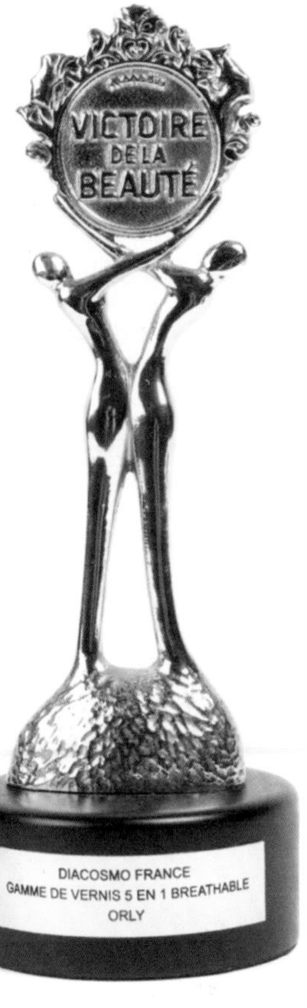
VICTOIRE
DE LA
BEAUTÉ
DIACOSMO FRANCE
GAMME DE VERNIS 5 EN 1 BREATHABLE
ORLY

The Award for Best Nail Lacquer 2018 for BREATHABLE Nail Color.

Jeff at the Casino de Paris receiving the
Victoire de la Beauté award, 2018.

Jeff with ORLY's French distributor,
Raymond Meyboom.

Nadia Deering, Vice President of International Sales with
Celebrity Manicurist/Ambassador Elsbeth Schutz, introducing
Builder in a Bottle. The Philippines, 2019.

Acknowledgments

Writing this book has given me the opportunity to recall all the wonderful people in my professional and personal life who have contributed in large and small ways to making this story come true.

I want to thank a few individuals who had a hand in helping me write what I hope will be an informative and an entertaining read. To Loren Stephens and Judy Chaikin of Write Wisdom, who listened to my stories and guided me in putting them on paper. To my former, long-time executive assistant, Shaina Martin, who kept me organized and freed me up during the time that I needed to focus on this book. And to my current executive assistant, Mya Stern, who had big shoes to fill and stepped into them with grace and efficiency. And to John Galea, Director of Public Relations, who pulled together the many photos that enhance the story of ORLY International.

And finally, to you, my readers—thank you for picking up this book. With luck, it will paint a portrait of what it takes to be an entrepreneur who has managed to endure through good times and bad for over forty years.

Jeff Pink's two closest friends within the beauty industry.

Jack Sperling and Jeff Pink.

Deborah Carver and Jeff Pink.

About the Author

As an ambitious young man who immigrated to the United States to study industrial management, Jeff Pink pursued the American dream of starting his own company and building it into a global beauty brand. With worldwide sales in sixty countries, ORLY is a family-owned business still helmed by Jeff with his three children, Ran, Tal, and Shanee working right alongside him.

To My Readers

Thanks for reading my book. Your feedback is important to me, so I'm hoping you'll take a moment to review it on Amazon.com.

www.orlybeauty.com.

IT ALL STARTED WITH
PINK

October 2019